Happy, Healthy Teens

Happy, Healthy Teens

Why Focusing on Relationships Works

Kari O'Driscoll

ROWMAN & LITTLEFIELD
Lanham • Boulder • New York • London

Published by Rowman & Littlefield
An imprint of The Rowman & Littlefield Publishing Group, Inc.
4501 Forbes Boulevard, Suite 200, Lanham, Maryland 20706
www.rowman.com

86-90 Paul Street, London EC2A 4NE, United Kingdom

Copyright © 2022 by Kari O'Driscoll

All rights reserved. No part of this book may be reproduced in any form or by any electronic or mechanical means, including information storage and retrieval systems, without written permission from the publisher, except by a reviewer who may quote passages in a review.

British Library Cataloguing in Publication Information Available

Library of Congress Cataloging-in-Publication Data

Names: O'Driscoll, Kari, author.
Title: Happy, healthy teens : why focusing on relationships works / Kari O'Driscoll.
Description: Lanham : Rowman & Littlefield, [2022] | Summary: "Happy, Healthy Teens uses what we know about adolescent brain and social development to offer concrete, actionable ideas to parents and educators as they seek to support and guide teens through the challenges of the middle and high school years"—Provided by publisher.
Identifiers: LCCN 2021038831 (print) | LCCN 2021038832 (ebook) | ISBN 9781475863796 (cloth) | ISBN 9781475863802 (paperback) | ISBN 9781475863819 (epub)
Subjects: LCSH: Teacher-student relationships. | Parent-teacher relationships. | Middle school students—Mental health. | High school students—Mental health. | Stress in adolescence. | Teenagers—Education—Psychological aspects.
Classification: LCC LB1033 .O25 2022 (print) | LCC LB1033 (ebook) | DDC 371.102/3—dc23
LC record available at https://lccn.loc.gov/2021038831
LC ebook record available at https://lccn.loc.gov/2021038832

To all the people in my life who have acted as parents to me, and to those who still do, thank you for offering me love and patience and teaching me what it is to be cared for unconditionally. Mom, I'm so sorry for the teenage years. To my daughters and their friends, thank you for allowing me to be part of your lives and learn from you as well. My life is so rich thanks to all of you amazing young people.

Contents

Acknowledgments ix

Introduction xi

1 Important Information about Adolescent Brain and Social Development 1
2 Mindfulness 21
3 Trusting Relationships 35
4 Compassion 59
5 Shared Goals 67
6 Conflict 77
7 Adolescent Health and Well-Being 89

About the Author 103

Acknowledgments

This book was made possible by a group of amazing writers whose work I follow and whose insights blow me away. The friends and family who have supported me through this research and been my guinea pigs as I tested new ideas are invaluable. I hope one day to be able to express my immense gratitude to all of them.

Introduction

Pretending that children only learn during the hours when they are at school is, at best, short-sighted and, at worst, dangerous. Pretending that, by the time they reach the teen years, they have learned the majority of what they need to know from their parents is also dangerous.

Adolescence is a time of rapid brain development and social identity formation. Unlike calculus or proficiency in a foreign language, many things that teens and tweens are learning during these years are hard to quantify or measure, but it doesn't make them any less important. Inside and outside of the classroom, not only are adolescents constantly taking in information, but their brains are tasked with streamlining and creating habits that they will rely on for the rest of their lives.

The kinds of things children learn at school are vastly different than the things they learn at home, and it can be a challenge for them to navigate different expectations and rules and cultural norms between the two places. When school staff and families aren't on the same page with regard to prioritizing tasks, what "work" looks like, and how curiosity is received, it is harder for everyone involved.

During the middle-school years, the focus often increases on helping children develop self-sufficiency. This can mean that parents and teachers are more alienated from each other and less able to form relationships. When teachers and family members don't communicate and share a common set of values, it is the youth who are tasked with constant code switching as they move from home to school and back.

The more parents and teachers share techniques and information, values and goals, the better off adolescents are because that helps them build a solid foundation from which to launch. That isn't to say that parents and teachers have to agree on everything, but agreeing on the most fundamental things—that we want the best for our children, that we see them as unique individuals who are worthy of our time and attention, that our job is to support them as they learn and grow—is vital.

It also means that teachers and parents need to learn to honor each other's expertise, perspectives, and hopes. Teachers can have unique insights into a child's learning style and challenges whereas parents can help fill in some of the details about why their students present the way they do. Learning from each other and collaborating on strategies to support teens and tweens is an important way to build a safe, strong container for youth as they tackle the challenges of moving through these years to become adults.

Teenagers have long been my favorite people. Their unique ability to have one foot in the world of childhood and one in adulthood makes them creative and positioned to access a way of being that isn't cynical or rigid. Their (sometimes frightening) willingness to take risks inspires me, and their bullshit detectors often lead me to question assumptions or beliefs I hold. Teenagers push me to think outside the box, be more playful, and remind me of the importance of close friendships outside my family unit.

And teenagers are under a lot of pressure. Not only are their bodies and minds changing in unpredictable and overwhelming ways, but the societal messages we send them about the importance of the choices they make during these years (while their brains are yet to be fully developed) can tip them into a place where they believe that every waking moment must be consumed with activity and productivity. What if you believed that every single choice you made right now had the power to impact the way the rest of your life went? Would you feel more fear about deciding whether to spend time with friends this weekend instead of working?

Adolescents' bodies require a lot of rest to support their intense growth, but we tell them they have to do well in school, excel in at least one extracurricular activity, take on more household responsibility, and start their school day often before 8 a.m. When teachers assign homework every day and other expectations pile up, often the day doesn't include enough hours to let youth sleep and regenerate. We are asking them to pit their physical and mental health against the expectations we and society have for them, and they can't win.

We often tell tweens and teens to "grow up," or come down on them for being immature and impulsive, but the truth is, they're wired that way. These years are about learning how to navigate their impulses and make good choices, and they have to make mistakes to do that.

So how can you, a parent or caregiver, mentor or loved one, support teens? How can you create a strong, loving connection to this young person that will help them stay emotionally healthy, learn to advocate for their own needs, and expand their network of trusted and trusting people? By forming a team of adults who can support each other and your children. We can't be expected to remember or even recognize all of the needs a young person has, but when we partner with teachers, coaches, and other caring adults, we can draw on each other's knowledge and strengths to come together and create space for children to grow up healthy and resilient.

This book will help you understand some of what is happening inside the teenage brain and body. The first chapter explains what is happening in the adolescent brain as well as how teens develop their own unique identity during these years. Knowing some of what is supposed to happen can give you context for why teens act in certain ways or the kinds of challenges they may be facing.

Adolescence is a confusing time, and it can be really impactful to help teens understand what's happening to them so that they can make choices with that knowledge. Talking with them about the unique challenges of this period of development is also a really great way to let them know that you acknowledge the pressure they're under and send the message that you're trying to help.

Subsequent chapters will look at how you can support the health and well-being of teens as they manage stress and anxiety, how to plant the seeds of a strong, reciprocal relationship (and avoid the barriers to trusting connections), and how you can provide a scaffolding as they navigate their educational journey.

The discussion topics and activities were designed to help you work with adolescents through some of the most challenging years you will face together. Based on the most current research on the adolescent brain and rooted in practical, tested ideas about how to connect with and nurture your child, it offers new ways to think about how to support our children as they grow up.

Whether or not we know it, parental relationships with our children are their first and most impactful examples of what relationships should be like, and the tempo we set for them as they stretch themselves further out into the world is incredibly important. And the teacher-student relationships formed during the adolescent years provide real-world practice at building supportive and caring networks.

As you make your way through this book, you will be encouraged time and again to really think about your ultimate goals with respect to adolescents you care about. Please take the time to ask yourself what kind of people you hope your children surround themselves with: those who respect their ideas and beliefs, or those who discount their ideas and worth and tell them what to do and how to live.

Think about whether you prefer children to think about relationships as power struggles or as fertile ground for collaboration and a safe exchange of ideas. Children learn more by watching us than they do by listening to us. Although we often wish they would do what we tell them to do, the fact is, they are more likely to do what we do, and they take their cues about self-worth from the way we talk to them. It is imperative that we treat them with respect and kindness.

It may sound simple, but it takes practice—especially if we weren't raised that way—and that is where this book comes in. It offers you a multitude of opportunities to practice interacting with teens and tweens with purpose, compassion, and respect.

If our children grow up with parents or caregivers who ignore their ideas and concerns and simply dictate how they should live and the choices they should make, how will they learn to go out into the world and be in relationship with people who treat them as equals?

Our first and most lasting lessons on relationships and navigating communication with others come from our families of origin, regardless of what they look like. We learn patterns of relating at home, so if we grow up with older siblings or parents who don't listen to us, shame and blame us, or use power tactics to control us, we will think that is normal and natural in our other loving relationships.

If we don't feel safe enough with our parents and siblings to express our true emotions and needs, we will struggle to make healthy connections with other people in our lives. We will believe that normal relationships are rooted in shame and blame and power differentials. If our school experiences normalize rigid authoritarianism, we learn to feel comfortable being controlled and seek out connections where we are not equal partners. Is that what we want for our children? Or do we want to give them opportunities to speak their truth, learn to advocate for themselves, and expect to be respected equally by partners and friends and coworkers?

Given the sheer number of hours that adolescents spend in school, the patterns they learn by interacting with other students reinforce many of their beliefs about how the world should be. As a teacher, you have an enormous impact on how youth experience social interactions and learn to work with people other than their family. It is not only the academic material, but the culture of your classroom and the individual relationship you have with students that will last for years to come.

Allowing bullying, shame, and divisions along class or race lines gives youth the impression that you feel powerless or that you don't care. Having difficult conversations and striving to create an atmosphere of care can counter many of the messages children get from the media and pop culture. Reaching out to families to create connections shows students that you see them as whole human beings and can offer you valuable insights into how to navigate those difficult conversations.

Thinking critically about how we interact with adolescents and what our goals are can make a big difference in the choices we make. By the time children reach adolescence, we often give them more responsibility without necessarily giving them more of our trust. For example, we may ask them to manage their own time, learn how to do their laundry, and pack their own lunch, but without letting them have some say in how or when those things happen. Even if they can't articulate it to us, this feels unfair to them, and they push back. And often, our response as adults is to shut them down.

Research shows that children who don't feel as though they are listened to or taken seriously tend to react in one of two ways: withdraw from the relationship or ratchet up their behavior in order to get attention. Most of us who work or live with adolescents can agree that both scenarios ultimately cause problems, so it's important to pay attention to our children and help them develop positive ways of being heard. In my experience, the most effective way to do that is with mindfulness.

Mindfulness has been demonstrated to increase resilience and flexibility, develop better self-control, help us set safe and healthy boundaries, problem solve, address stressful situations more effectively, and strengthen our relationships. Parents and teachers who nurture their children by acknowledging their needs and desires as well as helping them learn ways to address their needs decrease stress-related health issues for their children and support them in doing better academically.

Learning to pay attention to how we feel and react to things in our daily lives reminds us that we have the power to choose where we focus our thoughts and energies, and teaching our children to do the same sets positive patterns in place that will serve them for the rest of their lives.

Our job as parents and teachers is not to force our tweens and teens to do what we "know" is best for them. Our job is to help them decide whether something is important enough for them to choose to do it on their own. The fact is, "knowing" doesn't equal "doing." How many of us know that we will be healthiest if we exercise for thirty minutes a day? How many of us actually do that? How many of us know that we shouldn't text and drive? Drink too much alcohol? Get less than eight hours of sleep every night? And how many of us do (or refrain from) all of those things?

The trick is to help children link their values to their actions, to help them develop the internal motivation to do the things that are important to them. External motivations will only go so far, especially as we become more independent and come to realize that many of the reasons certain rewards were created was not because they were in our best interest, but in the interests of employers or teachers or other systems.

The truth is, human beings don't stick with anything for very long unless we really believe in the reasons for doing it—losing weight, quitting smoking, cooking healthy food, flossing our teeth. So, although it is faster and easier to motivate children by telling them what to do and punishing them if they don't listen to us, over time that approach doesn't help them become healthy, fully functioning adults, which is ultimately what we are supposed to be helping them achieve.

Mindfulness helps us understand our motivations and values and crystallize them so that we can act from our own choices and instincts more often rather than responding to external forces. Many of the activities and questionnaires in this book will ask you to reflect with care and really unpack some of the basic, bedrock beliefs you have that might not align with your goals for relationship with the teen or tween in your life. Modeling this kind of inquiry for youth is a powerful act and can have a really positive effect on your connection.

Chapter One

Important Information about Adolescent Brain and Social Development

Adolescence is a time of rapid growth and development. As a parent, no doubt, you've noticed your grocery bill rise along with your child's appetite. You've probably had to buy shoes more than once a year as your student outgrows pair after pair. You may greet your child in the kitchen or your student at school one morning and swear that she literally grew overnight.

What we can't see is that, during the years between the ages of ten and twenty, students' brains are developing just as rapidly and significantly as their bodies. Having information about what's happening and how can help us to parent and teach them in purposeful, effective ways.

Although they may be walking and talking and performing complicated tasks (such as designing a new business idea for school, or developing smartphone apps, or mixing their own music tracks), much of their important brain growth has yet to happen. Adolescents look like, sometimes sound like, and often demand to be treated like little adults, but it's important to remember that they're missing some vital pieces of the puzzle that take years to develop.

THE PREFRONTAL CORTEX

An area of the brain called the prefrontal cortex (PFC) won't be fully capable of performing all of its most complicated tasks for years, which is precisely what can make parents and teachers of middle- and high-school students so frustrated. The PFC is responsible for "executive functioning," tasks that include the ability to

- reason,
- solve problems creatively, and
- focus attention.

It takes a lot of practice over years to become fully capable of performing these complicated functions, which can be incredibly frustrating for everyone. But recognizing that these are things our children need to work on can help us be a little more patient with them. The good news is that the more we practice, the better we get. It is important to remember that expecting an adolescent to "act like an adult" is like asking a child to swim the length of the pool at his first swim lesson. It takes time and effort for them to build the skills needed to be adults.

It's also vital to realize that some things interfere with our ability to focus, solve problems, and reason. When we are tired, hungry, or have a strong emotional response to something, our PFC doesn't work very well. This has important implications for youth who routinely don't get enough sleep or enough to eat and for those who have experienced or are currently experiencing trauma.

The more we practice something under less than perfect conditions, the more likely we are to develop habits that undermine our ability to be healthy, so meeting our children's basic needs for food, rest, and emotional safety is the first step toward helping them create positive executive functioning. That is often easier said than done, and if it simply isn't possible, the least we can do is acknowledge the effect it has on their ability to function at the level we're asking them to.

I remember working with a class of about fifteen adolescents at an alternative high school for youth in recovery from addiction. Many of these students lived in difficult situations, to say the least, and I had to work to not take it personally when one young woman routinely came into the room, made herself comfortable on the couch, and slept through the entire ninety-minute session. The administrator was apologetic and offered to remove her from the classroom, but I told him it was clear that she was listening to her body and responding.

I would much rather reinforce that behavior than punish her or embarrass her. She obviously needed rest more than she needed my social-emotional skills class, and ultimately, learning to honor the cues your body is sending you about what it needs *is* socially and emotionally valuable, so she was learning something after all.

THE ROLE OF THE AMYGDALA

A key part of the brain, the amygdala, is highly active during the teenage years. This part of the brain is responsible for automatic emotional responses such as fear and aggression. It is also associated with conditioned responses (such as feeling hungry when you smell french fries, or flinching when you hear someone yelling) and motivation. During the adolescent years, the amygdala can swell to nearly three times the size of an adult's amygdala, which explains why in the teenage world emotions are often king.

This is partly why so many teens struggle with anxiety. The amygdala is pretty convincing when it senses danger, and even something that seems inconsequential to us (e.g., being made fun of by a teacher or peers) can feel paralyzing to an adolescent. The amygdala is responsible for our fight/flight/freeze responses and triggers a rush of adrenaline that can prompt an aggressive response, leave us speechless, or make us run away and hide. If you've ever watched someone make a decision based purely on emotion, especially if it seems out of proportion, you have seen just how powerful the amygdala is.

Most of us have, at one point or another, wanted something so badly that we created a logical justification for obtaining it. Tweens and teens are motivated by their desires as well, and without a fully developed prefrontal cortex, they lack the reasoning ability and the life experience to override their emotions and make healthy choices every time.

It is incredibly frustrating to question your children about why they did something and have them shrug and say, "I dunno," but more often than not, they are telling the truth. They *don't* know. It probably seemed like a good idea at the time, or at least not a horrible idea, but later, without the cloud of emotion they were feeling when they made that choice, it can be a mystery to them why they did what they did.

Emotions and thoughts are not separate entities in the human brain—the two are always interacting and influencing each other; when the brain reacts, it triggers physiological responses as well. If those responses cause physical discomfort (stomach pain, sweating, heart rate increase, flushing, etc.), the impulse to lash out or flee can be automatic.

When a teen's brain is flooded with emotion, it unleashes thoughts that may or may not be rational, and when those thoughts are rooted in fear, the circular response between emotion—thoughts—body reaction—emotion—thoughts—body reaction can be incredibly overwhelming. The body almost always will react even if we know we are safe. Think about the last time you watched a horror movie and something leaped out of the dark. You flinched, didn't you? You probably were able to interrupt the physiological response by reminding yourself that you were safe and just watching a movie—but not until after your body had responded on its own.

The human condition is such that we often experience our feelings as something we need to act on. This originated in the amygdala with our fight/flight/freeze response. But a little bit of practice taming the physiological response and taking the time to inquire about whether this situation really deserves a big reaction helps us connect to our prefrontal cortex and learn to make rational decisions. The more practice our children have at it during the adolescent years, the calmer they will be in their adult years when something goes awry.

This includes psychological fears as well. We all have had times when we worry about the way other people will see us or talk to us, but without a distinct effort to engage the rational brain, adolescents become prone to believe negative thoughts in their heads that are reinforced by their physical fear response. These thoughts can be things such as:

- *My life is terrible.*
- *Things will never get better.*
- *I am so stupid.*
- *Everyone hates me.*

Children who have a history of trauma are even less likely to be able to make rational connections that interrupt these self-defeating thoughts and painful emotions. Stress inhibits our ability to think rationally and learn, and our job as parents and teachers is to help children feel difficult emotions and practice dissecting the thoughts with intention so that they can create new thought patterns and find healthy ways to manage pain in the future.

This requires creating a feeling of safety and trust, which takes time. With repeated instances of calm, supportive responses, eventually adolescents can come to believe that they can have strong feelings without falling apart, and that once the most powerful emotions pass, they can begin to problem solve. Creating this kind of atmosphere at home and at school requires a concerted effort on the part of families and educators.

It is also important that we know when our children are feeling something really strong—anger, fear, sadness, or frustration—it is a bad idea to try to talk them out of it. The portion of the brain that controls language is different from the portion of the brain that controls decision making. So, even if we anticipate that our children are about to act on a strong feeling, and we think it's a bad idea, the lack of connection between the part of them that is processing our advice and the part that ultimately decides what to do—coupled with the overriding emotional response—means that we aren't likely to convince them to calm down by saying "you're blowing this out of proportion," or "if you just do X, it will all be fine."

When the amygdala is triggered, our ability to listen and really hear is compromised, and when we feel dismissed, we often respond by becoming more emotional. My daughters have told each other time and again that the worst thing they can hear when they are upset is, "Calm down!" That particular phrase often has the complete opposite effect and feels like gaslighting. But here is a way to help:

TIP: What to Do When Your Teens or Tweens Are "Freaking Out"

1. Acknowledge without judgment—let them know you see that they are upset, and it feels really powerful. The words you use here are as important as your body language. Remember, adolescents are "bullshit detectors," and they will know if you are patronizing them or you don't really mean it. Often, it is enough to simply say, "Oh, wow, this is a really difficult situation."

---

2. Encourage them to articulate what they are feeling—this activates the language center of their brain and will diminish some of the strong emotion *as long as they stick to describing what they're feeling and not spinning a story of why or what the fallout could be.*
3. Offer to help them test different scenarios. Activate the logic center of the brain as you help them think about whether this situation calls for a solution.* If it does, brainstorm ideas—even absurd ones (humor triggers creativity in many cases). This helps them practice processing strong emotions and sets up a pattern of asking for help from a trusted person when they're upset.

*Not all strong emotional responses require a solution. It is often enough to allow them to feel grief or rage, then work to accept the reality. It is hard for us to see children unhappy, but it is also important to discern whether a particular situation can be "fixed" and help them practice sitting with difficult emotions.

During these years, children can almost feel as though they're being held hostage by their mood swings. We have the opportunity to show them that they are not.

THE POWERFUL EFFECTS OF DOPAMINE

Another important piece of the adolescent brain puzzle is how sensitive the adolescent brain is to the neurotransmitter dopamine. Dopamine is involved with the brain's reward and pleasure centers. During the adolescent years, human beings require higher levels of dopamine in order to feel its effects, which means:

- dopamine gives teens and tweens a great emotional "high," and,
- over time, they build up a tolerance for it and require more and more of it to get the same feeling.

This is why children this age are driven to engage in risky behaviors. Unfortunately, coupled with their inability to make rational decisions (because the PFC is not yet fully developed), this can mean that they act impulsively, without stopping to consider the consequences. It also makes them more susceptible to addiction, because substances such as tobacco, alcohol, and illegal drugs trigger dopamine production, flooding their brains with a potent reward when they use them.

We can use other things that trigger dopamine production to our advantage. One is pattern recognition. When our brains "figure out" something, dopamine is released. Often, when we are told a story that helps us understand a complicated idea, we get a little emotional "high." Stories have also been shown to prompt our brains to release oxytocin and cortisol, two hormones that decrease stress and increase our ability to connect with others, which is why adolescents can build such strong relationships with people who share their interests.

That doesn't mean that we should spend all our time telling children stories about our lives at their age, but it does mean that reading books together and discussing them, watching movies together, and playing games is a great way to spark connection and conversation with children and help them feel good.

This can be a great way to direct adolescents toward healthy things and to understand why video games, for example, are so enticing. Video games give children a way to solve puzzles within stories, and the dopamine hit they get from conquering a digital foe or getting to the next level is just as real as one they get from anything else.

Helping tweens and teens find healthy ways to experience the high of solving a complex problem and think critically about the stories we hear to determine whether they are real is something we can do for teens that will have lasting impacts. It is a great way to motivate students to engage in complex problems that they may not think are useful or important. Explaining context and purpose and encouraging them to explore it from different angles with a partner whose interests are similar can give them a way to try something that they wouldn't otherwise.

Sometimes, as parents, when we ask our children about their classes and schoolwork, they assume we're asking because we want to monitor their progress, and they become defensive. Asking them to show you what they're working on or teach you a concept they just learned can help them integrate the information and get an emotional high as their brain solves the puzzle again. It's important not to judge, though; remember, children this age know when we're being patronizing or trying to manipulate them.

NEUROPLASTICITY

Perhaps neuroplasticity is the most promising thing we have going for us during these difficult years. This basically means that we all have the ability to impact the way our brains work over time, but this is especially true during the teen years. It is believed that neuroplasticity is at an all-time high during the adolescent years, meaning that the brain's ability to set patterns of thinking that will serve for decades is enormous.

Dr. Dan Siegel describes this phenomenon as building the brain's superhighways—laying the groundwork in the adolescent years that helps us make good choices, rely less on impulsive acts that are reward driven, and think creatively will mean that over time, all of those things require much less effort. We don't have to continually blaze those trails as we get older if we do the work during the teenage years.

Working with adolescents to emphasize slowing down to let emotions dissipate before acting, using critical thinking to tackle challenges, and integrating information from different sources helps them develop those superhighways. We need our PFC to deal with unexpected situations, to concentrate, and to be flexible, and learning that during these years will ultimately increase our efficiency and decrease stress.

Parents and teachers can create an environment that encourages children to practice these executive functions. When we are tired, hungry, lonely, stressed, or sad, we don't filter and process information as well. We tend to stay stuck in our emotions and have a hard time using our PFC. If a teen or tween has a hard time focusing or is getting frustrated, take a minute to assess whether he needs a snack or a break to do something fun. Normalizing this kind of response to your body's cues is important to help children understand their unique needs and it often increases their ability to integrate information.

In subsequent chapters, you will learn important ways to help by modeling mindfulness and compassion, using empathy instead of shame, creating shared goals, dealing with conflict in productive ways, and dealing with stress and anxiety, which can be incredibly overwhelming for children this age.

Brain development is shaped by consistent, supportive relationships, responsive communication, and modeling. Starting to develop the habitual responses of slowing down, paying attention to our children when they need us, and responding thoughtfully and with support is important because it keeps their brains from being hijacked by their feelings by integrating their emotional reactions into their thought processes and behavior choices.

In order for children to learn, they need social and emotional support. Positive, loving relationships create the optimal environment for integrating new information, whereas fear, anxiety, and self-doubt decrease our capacity to learn. We can literally turbocharge brain development by slowing down and supporting adolescents emotionally and teaching them to listen to their own needs.

Most of us weren't parented or taught this way, and it can be challenging to train ourselves to respond in this manner, especially if a child's behavior or choices inspire fear or anger in us. It is a process that requires time, intentionality, and compassion, and the goal is not to do it perfectly but with transparency. Giving children opportunities to practice acknowledging their emotions and using that information to more fully understand themselves and make deliberate choices is a powerful way to embed patterns of thinking and relating that will mean they are able to manage challenges in the future.

SOCIAL IDENTITY

Many of the most challenging problems parents and teens experience come down to issues of identity. Our sense of identity can include gender, race, ethnicity, sexual orientation, socioeconomic status, religion, nationality, physical/cognitive ability, primary interests, and much more. It is tremendously complex and evolves over time, and often it is informed by our family, rules of society, and cultural traditions.

Our social identity is influenced by things that aren't changeable or chosen (the color of our skin, our gender and sexuality, our family culture, etc.), but it also includes things we choose to use to express to others who we are. Although we can't always directly link these things, if I am more comfortable in groups of people and can easily express myself verbally, my social identity will reflect that. If I am more introverted and comfortable observing to learn, I may dress in a more conservative way so I do not stand out, I may choose roles that are supportive rather than traditional leadership roles, and I may prefer to spend time with one or two people instead of a large gathering.

During the adolescent years, children begin to be more influenced by people outside their immediate family and explore ideas of who they are at their core. They can begin to question their values and passions and how they align with or are different from their parents. This can feel threatening for families and frightening for teens and tweens, and often teachers get caught in the middle. Pico Iyer says that we often see people "through the keyhole of our own priorities," and it is often difficult to separate our hopes and dreams for our children from the people they are. This is where teachers and parents can support each other.

Educators and nonfamily members can be free to have a more expansive view of teens and tweens because it doesn't necessarily threaten their priorities or values or sense of self when a young person doesn't share their views. When parents and teachers can talk about who a child is on the whole, it can help alleviate some of the biggest fears parents have about their child's developing identity. In a strong, open relationship, parents and teachers can be honest with each other without dumping their fears on the young person who is already burdened with a lot of questions and dilemmas.

The reason this process is so frustrating and scary is because a profound tension exists between one's identity and the need to belong. Human beings are designed to live in community and to feel as though they are an accepted member of a tribe, and it is important for each of us to feel grounded and settled in who we are as individuals. Knowing what we value, how we see ourselves, and what is most important to us as we make our way in the world can see us through challenging times, and if the way we define who we are threatens our place in our chosen community or family unit, it can be really frightening.

Part of an adolescent's job during these years is to "try on" different ways of being. For some children, this means hair dye and a budding interest in art. It is perfectly normal for children who was always a natural athlete to show interest in spending time pursuing other interests during adolescence. They may bounce from activity to activity for a while trying to find something they are passionate about. Their taste in music or clothes may change, and people who were their close friends for years may fall away to be replaced by new people parents don't know as well.

It's important to see this for what it is and lead with curiosity, rather than longing for "the good old days" or judging children's choices. Maybe your child played soccer during the elementary years to please you or because it had some social benefit, but now that he is beginning to explore what he'd really like to do, soccer might not feel as compelling as choir.

During these years, teens are beginning to test their relationships with others outside the family. It's important that they develop the skills to discern who is reliable, trustworthy, and supportive, so that when they go out on their own, they can build community for themselves. Letting them experiment while you can still be the safety net when things fall apart is a great way to let them take small steps toward creating strong relationships later.

It can feel scary, but it is important as adults that we spend time trying to assess whether their experiments are dangerous or simply make us uncomfortable. It may well be that your children will join the choir and decide that it's not for them, after all. Or they may discover a new passion and talent that wouldn't have surfaced if they hadn't had the courage to try. And you may learn from your children's school counselor or homeroom teacher that they seem happy and content at school, even if you're upset with their new friend group.

It is important to know that although some choices won't last into adulthood (who among us didn't have a "goth" or "punk" phase), they are no less valid and real for that young person at the time. Trusting individuals to know themselves best is a powerful endorsement of their right to their own thoughts and feelings, no matter how uncomfortable it makes us. Our job as adults is to give children the space to practice choosing and learning what happens as a result while keeping them safe and reminding them that we care about them, no matter what.

The human brain has adapted over time to incorporate social and emotional well-being into its idea of what we need to survive. Because we are social beings who exist and thrive in community, we are keenly aware that our status in community is vital to our continued existence. Nobody feels that more deeply than adolescents, both because they are more aware of and responsive to their emotions than adults and because they are deep in this process of developing their identities.

When we as adults are disdainful or judgmental of what children say is important to them and a vital part of who they are, we are telling them they are not worthy of our respect as whole human beings. Making fun of their clothes, friends, hobbies, and interests is more harmful than we think, because those are important ways that they express their passions and values. When we tell them they are unacceptable or reject them because of their gender identity or sexuality, we are sending the message that only under certain conditions will we accept and love them.

Telling children that something is wrong with them—whether in so many words or by mocking or shaming them—is not a recipe for a healthy, loving relationship; it is an outright rejection of who they are in that moment. Revealing your true self is a vulnerable act, and we owe it to them to recognize that. The effect of rejecting someone when they tell us who they think they are—even if it changes over time—lasts and can make it nearly impossible to create trust.

When tweens and teens are able to play with identity within the context of a loving family and community, the consequences aren't as overwhelming, and they can experiment without worrying that they will lose a sense of belonging. But when those experiments result in rejection from parents or siblings or extended family, it can set up a dynamic where the young person doesn't feel like they can trust themselves to know what feels good to them. Often, the act of trying things on is the best way for a young person to know what feels right, and the freedom to do that and still know they are loved and accepted sets them up to believe in themselves and develop their instincts.

The rifts created in families during this time can be tremendously painful. Although we may think our children know that we love them, no matter what, we can act in ways that make them feel as though we don't. In her book *All about Love: New Visions*, bell hooks writes that in order for us to be in relationship with each other, we have to agree on a sense of shared reality. If we can't agree on what is real and important, we have no foundation for a loving relationship.

If I tell you that I am gay, and you say that, first and foremost, I am part of my family's religious tradition—which says that I can't be religious *and* gay—we don't have a shared reality. And if you are my parent and, as such, in a position of power over me, I am then forced to choose between your version of reality and mine. That means that I am forced to choose between belonging to our family, if belonging means I accept your truth, and belonging to myself, if I truly believe that I am gay. If, instead, our shared reality is around mutual respect and care for each other, my identity doesn't threaten my belonging. I can be gay and still be part of the tribe.

Because adolescents inherently know how important belonging is, they use it as a weapon against each other in school and social settings. If membership in the tribe is also threatened at home, youth can feel increasingly desperate and frightened. If as parents we want our children to develop a strong sense of self and an unshakable belief in their values, we have to set aside our discomfort and judgment in favor of unconditional love and remind them that they will always be welcome in our family.

If you are having a particularly difficult time navigating this, it may be helpful to seek therapy or work through some of the following questions on your own or with a trusted friend:

> ACTIVITY: My Identity Development
>
> 1. What was my social identity development like as a teenager? What did I experiment with, and how was it received by my parents?
> 2. What are some of my most closely held values? When did I know that they were important to me?
> 3. What about my child's ideas and actions threatens my sense of who I am as a parent and a person?
> 4. What are my biggest fears regarding my child's experimentation with identity? Are they realistic? Where did they come from?

I encourage teachers and other school personnel to do that activity as well, because you are often some of the most powerful allies for students who don't have support at home or in their social networks. Any validation by a trusted adult of children's right to figure out who they are at their core is a way to insulate them from the deep self-doubt and negative self-image that can emerge during these years.

Often, our reaction to students who are "different" reflects our own deeply held beliefs about identity and is informed by culture, family, religion, and other institutional systems that can keep us from focusing on the health and well-being of young people. Knowing that the best learning happens within the context of safe, caring relationships, we can shift our perspective to creating connections with youth that feel authentic and have a huge impact.

When human beings are stressed, they seek immediate safety, and often that means going back to what is comfortable and "known." This isn't a recipe for growth or learning; it keeps us small and afraid. The best way to encourage growth is to let children know they are safe with us and that we have their backs, no matter what. Stunting teens' identity development to suit our preferences won't keep them from being a certain way; it only prevents them from expressing it to make us feel comfortable, which, ultimately, is traumatic and erodes our relationship with them and their relationship to themselves.

ABSTRACT THINKING

One of the most amazing things the adolescent brain does is to begin developing the ability to synthesize ideas and information in an abstract way across seemingly unconnected domains. This means that, where once they were only able to see things in black and white/right and wrong, tweens and teens are now able to appreciate nuances and shades of gray. A big part of this involves asking lots of questions, but not in the same way they did when they were two, in that never-ending series of "why?"

More often than not, when tweens and teens want more information, it comes in the form of pushback, challenging ideas and people in authority, and trying to understand systems and processes. Remember, they get a big dopamine hit when they solve a puzzle or put together information in a way that makes sense to them, so they are literally driven to seek this kind of knowledge, even if the way they do it feels disrespectful to you.

When adolescents are encouraged to push boundaries and think outside the box, the results can be awesome. Teens have invented such things as a pedal-powered water purifier for use in third-world countries, and devices that collect plastic in the oceans and alert caregivers when a patient with dementia wanders off. Because they still have one foot in the world of childhood where imagination rules and one foot in the adult world of problem solving with practicality, their brains are uniquely positioned to come up with ideas that are exciting and new.

Questioning established norms and rules is both incredibly exciting and creative and often experienced as inappropriate to parents and teachers. But we can navigate this in a way that helps our children nurture creative problem-solving skills and inquire with positive, productive intent.

It can be aggravating when children challenge rules about curfew or chores or assignment deadlines, but if we want them to grow up being able to question seemingly arbitrary, outdated rules at work or college, it's our job to teach them how to do it in a respectful way.

Expect teens to challenge you, and find a way to turn the challenge into a conversation. They may be asking out of sincere curiosity, not because they don't recognize your wisdom and authority. Meet their curiosity with curiosity, and you might be surprised at their ability to come up with creative solutions that help everyone. I sometimes reflect on instances where my own children inspired me to challenge what I thought was possible or a given with gratitude that they opened up my mind to new ways of being. This is one of the most awesome things about the adolescent brain, and with the proper care and nurturing, this kind of thinking can last for the rest of their lives.

TRAUMA

With every passing day, we learn more about trauma and its effects on the brain and our social interactions. Many of us have experienced trauma in our lives that shaped the way we think about ourselves and others, as well as how we react to unexpected events. Having and/or working with children often shines a spotlight on ways we have learned to cope (or not) and can bring out powerful emotions or thought and behavior patterns that we don't expect.

Many of our children have also experienced trauma, and it's important to understand how it affects the way we move through the world. Teachers come into contact with youth who have experienced and are currently experiencing trauma every single day, and it can be triggering and overwhelming to understand how to have a positive impact on them.

Simply put, trauma has a big impact on our ability to be in relationship. It's also critical to note that everyone responds to trauma in a slightly different way. Some people who witness or experience cruelty or violence are more likely to cling to others and see them as necessary for survival, whereas others react by pushing people away and becoming hyper-individuated, determined to rely only on themselves.

Regardless of the behaviors we develop as a response to trauma, our brains respond by making associations and trying to make sense of events, and our bodies react by becoming more receptive to certain hormones and increasing or decreasing certain bodily functions.

All of this means that our immediate response to an unexpected event or strong emotions may prevent us from connecting to others around us in such a way that we can accurately assess the threat and open our brains to learn from this new situation. The most powerful thing we as adults can do is help our children learn to regulate their nervous system when their trauma is triggered so that they can access the logic and listening centers of their brain. The best way to do that is to understand first how we can regulate our own nervous systems when we are with a young person who is having a trauma response.

> ACTIVITY: Co-Regulation and Emotional Attunement
>
> When your child is triggered and having a trauma response, having a calm, loving adult sit with him and help him get back to a place of calm is extremely important. These three steps can interrupt the physiological (body) response and help him feel more in control:
>
> 1. Breathe in for a count of four, hold that breath for a count of four, exhale for a count of four, hold that breath for a count of four. Repeat three more times.
> 2. While continuing to breathe slowly and regularly, repeat the mantra (out loud or in your head): I am safe. I am loved. I am here.
> 3. Feel your feet on the ground. Touch the chair or the ground you're sitting on with your entire palm and fingers. Continue breathing slowly and regularly.

The activities above work because the part of the brain that registers feelings is adjacent to the part that regulates body temperature and breathing. Focusing on our breath has a direct impact on our heart rate and other autonomic nervous system activities. The mantra takes advantage of the fact that, while our minds are almost always either looking to the past or the future, our bodies can only ever exist in this present moment. When we focus on our bodies, both by acknowledging that we are safe and here and by feeling our physical surroundings with our hands and feet, it is a reminder that in this moment, we are safe and not threatened.

With or without a trauma history, our primary goal is to feel safe at all times. When we don't feel safe, our limbic system kicks in to optimize our body's responses in case we need to fight or run away. This increases our heart rate and breathing and shuts down our digestive system and prefrontal cortex. When we feel these bodily sensations, we can feel validated in our worry that we're not safe.

As an adult, when you notice a child is having a fear response, if you believe that he is truly safe in that moment, helping him calm the physiology will have the effect of calming his mind as well. Help him understand what will make him believe that he is safe in that particular moment.

Routes of Safety, Adapted from Work by Jake Ernst, MSW RSW

The most fundamental building block of any strong relationship is the ability to feel safe with another person. To communicate effectively, feel heard, collaborate, and calm our nervous system enough to access our higher executive functions, we have to feel we are in a place where we belong (or could belong), where our gifts are acknowledged, and where we are supported as we meet our challenges.

If we are fearful of being mocked, rejected, or ignored, we cannot show up as our full, creative selves. Human beings are wired to be in relationship and designed to seek out spaces where we feel we belong. Environments that include power dynamics and hierarchical structures often mean that our "belonging" is contingent on decisions that those who have power over us make, which hinders our ability to be in relationship with others.

When we work to help each other feel safe sharing our ideas and experiences, we open up opportunities for collaboration and shared success, but depending on our individual lived experience, we all have different needs and "routes" to safety.

Spending some time figuring out what things help us feel calm and cared for is an important step to building relationship. Once we know our own route to safety, we can share that information with others and invite them to understand how best to support us.

We can also inquire about their preferences and begin to interact within a system of care that strengthens our connection to each other. This doesn't mean that we interrogate each other's reasons for needing certain things to feel safe, and it doesn't mean we judge routes that are different from our own. Acceptance is key.

Below are different "routes to safety" with descriptions designed to help you determine your needs when you feel vulnerable.

- Inner Guidance—using your own knowledge and somatic cues to find safety. Can include journaling, meditation, self-compassion, re-

peating affirmations. Often requires removing yourself from others for a while in order to find clarity. Nature can be a positive way to access this groundedness within yourself.
- Structure and Certainty—using logic and concrete information to find safety. Can include creating a list or schedule, tidying up your physical space and organizing, focusing on breaking things down into small pieces and setting aside big-picture concerns for the moment. Often requires asking others to refrain from catastrophizing or projecting best/worst case scenarios and focusing on tasks that are accomplishable in the immediate future.
- Sensory Experience—using sensory and somatic cues to regulate the nervous system and find safety. Can include deep breathing, squeezing a stress ball, taking a walk, eating your favorite food. Often requires a quiet place with no outside distractions and being surrounded by soothing objects (favorite scented candle, worry stone, photos of nature, soothing music).
- Relationship—using connections to others to create sense of safety. Can include conversation with active listening, physical touch to indicate connection, spoken affirmations, careful attention to body language and tone of voice, focusing on compassion and shared understanding. Often requires co-regulation with one specific person. People with this route to safety fear isolation or 'banishment" when they are upset or triggered. (Some people will be able to co-regulate with physical touch, and others will feel threatened by it. Before reaching out, ask your child if he wants a hug or an arm around his shoulders.)
- Protective Measures—using boundaries and coping mechanisms to find safety. Can include asking for repair if you feel triggered, speaking your truth firmly and clearly, identifying a physical mechanism (eating, smoking, taking a walk) that will calm your nervous system. Can look demanding or rigid and often needs to be fine-tuned to help individuals self-advocate without blaming others.
- Common Humanity—using shared experiences to connect and co-regulate to find safety. Can look like reminiscing about a good memory, making a joke to ease tension, tuning in to someone else's discomfort and asking if they OK, complimenting someone, or reestablishing a personal connection.

These routes are not mutually exclusive, nor are they necessarily static. As we build relationship with others, we can change our needs over time, or we may have different routes to safety with different people, but being aware of what helps us feel safe can give us the foundation we need to speak openly and honestly with our loved ones.

Once you're aware of what makes you feel safe, you can begin to inquire about other important people in your life. You may discover that assumptions you made about your partner or child are based on your personal route to safety. Encourage the adolescents in your life to explore what makes them feel safe. They may or may not choose to share that information with you, depending on the strength of the connection between you.

Chapter Two

Mindfulness

> Our kids only know they have something to say if someone listens to them.—Gloria Steinem

Mindfulness has many different definitions, but I describe it as the simple act of paying attention to what is going on in your head and your body. The word I most associate with mindfulness is curiosity. If we can take a moment to ask ourselves

- what is happening right now,
- how is it affecting me, and
- why is it affecting me this way,

we are being mindful.

Any time you notice that you are particularly emotional about something—whether that emotion shows up as anger or sadness or anything in between—and you can stop for a moment without lashing out or building a story around it, you are being mindful. Although it takes practice, we can practice paying attention to our children and being mindful with them in many simple ways that make a big difference.

Mindfulness has important benefits for all of us. Research shows that practicing mindfulness helps us

- control our impulses,
- understand our emotions and how they affect us physically,

- develop empathy and compassion for ourselves and others, and
- modulate our stress responses.

Often, mindfulness is accompanied by breathing techniques, and with good reason. Focusing on deep breathing decreases heart rate, raises body temperature, and balances the neurotransmitters in the brain. This means we are more likely to feel relaxed and alert, and we can focus and think clearly. Over time, you may find that an intention to be more present is automatically coupled with a deeper, slower breath.

So how does this impact your relationships with adolescents? Profoundly, and with a few simple tweaks.

Mindfulness can be as simple as looking up and making eye contact when your child enters the room. It can be hard to tear ourselves away from the computer screen or dinner prep, sweeping the floor or tending to another child, but acknowledging your adolescent when she walks into the room is a powerful tool.

We all know what it feels like to say hello or ask someone a question and have them respond without even looking up at us. The message it sends is that we aren't important enough for them to stop what they're doing. If you can't stop what you're doing or interrupt a phone conversation, you can at least make eye contact as a way to acknowledge a child's presence when he enters the room.

Taking this a step further, it is vital that we examine the messages we send our children with our habitual responses to them. Remember that every interaction during the teen years is first processed in the emotion center of the brain (the amygdala), so our words and actions are incredibly important.

FIRST IMPRESSIONS

When you first see your children in the morning as everyone is rushing around to get ready for work and school, what do you say? Do you comment about their uncombed hair or dirty/short/inappropriate clothing? Do you launch into reminders of what time it is and how much is left to accomplish before they can leave? Do you interrogate them about whether they finished their homework and if their soccer clothes are packed for later?

As a teacher, what is your first interaction with students like, especially if one approaches you with a problem and needs help? If the first thing you say relates to their physical appearance or timeliness, that sets the tone for the rest of the time you'll spend with them.

Sarcasm can feel like a "cool" way to connect with students, but if it is at another student's expense, the message it sends is one of judgment, so if you want students to trust you and feel as though you're their partner in learning, they can't be worried that they might be a target for your jokes at some point.

All of this is normal, common, and a dismissal of who a child is at her core. When we first note someone's physical appearance, it says that the way the world sees them is more important than who they are. It says that we are less interested in the potential for conversation than what they're wearing today.

When we start by commenting on someone being late or loud or reminding them of the things they need to do, it sets up the interaction as transactional instead of relational. It reinforces the notion that their accomplishments or actions are the thing we are most interested in.

The antidote to that is to stop, make eye contact, and smile. This simple act of being acknowledged by someone who is truly happy to see them helps them internalize the message that they are loved. Taking a moment to stop what you're doing and really notice a child also gives you the space to respond independent of what you were doing when they came into the room. I call this "taking your emotional temperature."

ACTIVITY: Taking Your Emotional Temperature

When we are annoyed—stuck in traffic, or paying bills, or reading a nasty e-mail from the boss—we react to everyone around us a little less calmly. If you're feeling rushed and frustrated when your child enters the room to ask a favor or tell you he'll be late after practice tonight, you are more likely to react negatively even if what he is saying isn't truly a problem. Stopping for a beat to acknowledge and set aside your frustration with the other situation can help you shift gears to be fully present with your child and set a different tone for the interaction. That is mindfulness.

Close your eyes and take in a deep breath. Exhale through your mouth. Think about the primary emotion you're feeling right now. It can be hard to separate them if you're feeling a mix of emotion at the moment, so just notice which ones show up.

> Bored, anxious, worried, restless, sad, peaceful, happy, angry, frustrated—just let the words float in your mind. Does one stand out more than the others? Try not to get caught up in the story behind the emotions, or explain why, or try to figure it out. Just note what you're feeling. If one stands out, try to focus on it and see where it lands in your body. If you're angry or frustrated, maybe it shows up as a tightness in your chest. If you're happy, maybe you have a warm glow in your belly. Don't think about why you feel the way you do or judge whether it's good or bad, just notice.
>
> When you're ready, take a deep breath and open your eyes. Write down the top two or three emotions you were feeling. That is your emotional temperature. At any given time, we all feel a mix of things, but generally one or two are more prevalent.

So why does emotional temperature matter? Our brains react so quickly to situations we're in that, often, we aren't paying attention to the emotions that color our responses. Think about how slowly things move when it's cold. Imagine your thoughts and words as honey. When your emotional temperature is cool (peaceful, joyful, happy, content), you are more likely to react to a new or unexpected situation with curiosity and optimism. It is as if you are wearing rose-colored glasses that see everything as glass half full. You are less likely to jump to conclusions and more likely to make rational, reasoned choices.

When it's warm, honey flows more quickly. If you're feeling anxious or fearful, angry or frustrated, you are more likely to assume bad intent or negative outcomes, or be unwilling to give someone the benefit of the doubt. Your reactions are swift and decisive and often, emotionally driven, as if you're wearing dark glasses that see shadow instead of light.

When our emotion centers are activated by anger or sadness or fear, the logic center of our brain is less able to do what it does best, and the portion of our brain that processes language (i.e., hears what people are saying and processes it accurately) can shut down. We literally don't listen to other people as well when we are upset.

When a child comes to you with a challenge or request, take a second to assess your emotional temperature. Often, other things going on around us lead us to react in ways that are inappropriate or disproportionate to the situation. When we are grieving, we are more irritable and quicker to anger. When we are tired or anxious, we tend to respond negatively to others. This activity gives you a way to remember that even if you're having a stressful day, you can choose to respond after setting those emotions aside.

WORDS MATTER

Mindfulness also involves taking care with the words we use when we talk about our children. The human brain loves a shortcut, and we use them often in our language. We create nicknames and labels for people so that we can generalize and make decisions more quickly. A lot of the time, that's beneficial, but when it comes to children, it can create barriers to connection or lead to assumptions about their motivations or desires that aren't true. By the time they hit the teen years, we've had years and years to form opinions about who they are and what makes them tick.

Remember, adolescence is a time when children are stretching themselves, trying on new identities, and expanding their ideas of who they are. They don't necessarily want to stay in those little boxes we built around them, so it's important to examine the things we think we "know" about them. Even if we think we are letting them explore new ways to interact with the world, we don't always give them the freedom to do that.

We make assumptions based on what we think we "know" about them (the oldest is the "clever, crafty one," and the youngest is the "wild child who doesn't look before she leaps"), and we often react to them from that place without thinking. This can show up in school when teachers pass along information on students to their next year's teacher. Be careful when you read someone else's assessment of a child; be aware that their impressions might be colored by their own perspective.

Each of us is a complex human being, which is a really good reason why families and teachers forming closer connections is good for youth. The more we can share information about how we see a child in different situations, the more we can see them as whole humans instead of stereotypes. You might be surprised to hear that this really shy child has a wicked sense of humor and a spectacular curve ball. And you might see him a little differently and more full of possibility than you did before.

ACTIVITY: Labels

What if we step back and challenge stereotypes about our children a little bit? Instead of boxing someone into a narrow place where they might not be happy, we can send a message of tolerance and curiosity. Try asking yourself these four questions the next time you jump to conclusions about a child's motivations or values:

1. What am I assuming about my child right now, and is it true?

At this point, it is natural for our brains to jump right into rationalizing and listing supporting evidence for our assumptions. "Of course, she is the wild child! Look how many broken bones she's had. Remember the time she moved all the furniture around and broke the bookshelf?" Take note of what happens when you ask the question, "Is it true?"

2. Can I think of other instances that counteract this label?

Couldn't she really be athletic and determined to give 110 percent, which accounts for the broken bones? Are there times when she has done something really risky and pulled it off brilliantly? Can I think of times when she was appropriately cautious? What if "wild child" is really "courageous"?

3. What is my gut reaction to the assumption I'm making?

Am I disgusted because she is nothing like I am, or frightened because I acted exactly like that at that age, and it got me into trouble? What is my deep emotional response to her? Could it have an impact on how I treat her when she makes a mistake?

4. What happens if I let go of the label and try to see this child as a person with many different attributes and abilities?

How might she respond if I drop the label and see her through a different lens? How might my reactions to her be different the next time she comes to me with a problem? Would our interaction be more satisfying and productive if I ask questions about why she makes certain choices instead of acting on the assumption?

Some common labels we use to describe kids include:

- clown
- perfectionist
- scaredy-cat
- control freak
- introvert/extrovert
- fearless
- scattered
- show-off
- airhead
- jock
- princess
- bookworm

Ample evidence may support one or more of those labels, but when we use them so often that we convince ourselves we "know" someone, we can trick ourselves into making assumptions about their motivations and their potential. We may end up setting expectations for them that they don't feel they can escape, and we stop listening to them, which makes them stop talking to us.

Evidence shows that when we think we already know the answer or outcome, we don't really pay attention to anything else. But letting children have the freedom to try out new attitudes and interests can encourage them to break free of rigid stereotypes and let them know that we see that they are capable of so many different things. The world will place limits on them in so many ways, the least we can do as trusted adults is remove any we've created.

One other thing to note is that when we label children in certain ways (jock versus bookworm), they may use that as an excuse to not try new things. Someone who has been called a jock his whole life may not believe he will ever be good at academic pursuits, and those who are known as "bookworms" may be reluctant to try athletic endeavors, even if they want to.

Sit down with your children and ask what labels they hear used about them. Do they know where those come from? Do they feel justified? Does your child feel trapped or defined by these labels? Encourage them to talk about how they're affected by or use these names to define themselves, and ask if they'd like to be known for something else, or if there is something they've outgrown.

You could start the conversation by thinking back to your own childhood and adolescence and identifying labels you wish you could shed. Were the labels at home different from the ones at school? Are there labels placed on you now that you think limit your ideas of how to behave and choices you could make? How does that feel?

DELIBERATE PARENTING CHOICES

> Love is the will (choice) to nurture our own and another's spiritual growth. Simply giving care does not equal loving. Genuine love is a combination of care, commitment, trust, knowledge, responsibility, respect, and an open, honest expression of all of the above.—bell hooks

We all love our kids, but there's a difference between loving someone and being invested in them as individuals (and not for how they reflect on who we are). The quote from bell hooks may feel incredibly overwhelming, but it boils down to making deliberate choices about how we relate to our children. Succumbing to knee-jerk responses that are often informed by the way we were parented or taught by others is not generally a healthy way of relating to our children.

When we rule with fear, we teach children that the world is a scary place; beyond that, it's hard to build trust with someone who is afraid of us. Children need to attach securely to an adult to move out into the world with confidence, but it is impossible to feel secure in a relationship where you have no power and you are not treated with kindness and reverence and compassion. Secure attachment builds trust, and although it is often easier and quicker to control behavior with threats, it doesn't help build a vision of a world that is safe to explore.

So how do we lead with care and love? How do we choose kindness and reverence and compassion? How do we make deliberate choices that show young people we are prioritizing their growth and learning and not just following rules? We have to keep in mind their strengths and challenges. We have to think about what we're asking of them and discern whether it aligns with their development.

When children are young, we often ask and/or expect them to do things that are developmentally unreasonable. We tell them to be silent, sit still, not forget things. Young children aren't physiologically designed to do any of those things, and yet we often punish them for not being able to.

This pattern continues as children get older. When youth hit the adolescent years, we often use isolation as a punishment (grounding, taking away phone privileges, suspension), prevent them from taking risks, tell them not to argue or ask questions or challenge us, and expect them to remember all the things they are supposed to do and have with them at any given time. Looking back to the first chapter on adolescent brain development, we can see how this approach flies directly in the face of who adolescents are and how they are built physiologically.

Teens need social interaction, they are driven to take risks, their brains are designed to question and create meaning from complex ideas, and their prefrontal cortex is not fully developed. When we know better, we do better, as Maya Angelou said. Making deliberate choices about how to interact with and motivate adolescents is a combination of our loving them and knowing what they need from us as trusted adults.

But old habits die hard, and we may hear the voice of parents or elders in our heads as we try to determine how to speak to our teens and tweens. When we are emotionally activated—angry or frustrated or fearful—we don't think straight and often revert to phrases or actions that we learned from others when we were young without determining whether they make sense in this instance.

ACTIVITY: What Is My Parenting Bias?

We all have conditioned responses and internal biases, and it can be hard to acknowledge or even understand what those are when it comes to parenting. Looking at them can feel threatening to our relationship with our own parents, but it doesn't have to be. This can help you think differently about why you respond the way you do to your child. Start by asking yourself the following questions without judgment. No answer is right or wrong: this is about gathering information so that you can respond to your teenager in an intentional way. Think about the answers from the perspective of you as a child and compare them to your life now. What is different? What might you be holding on to that isn't relevant to your child's experiences?

1. What was the makeup of my family as a child? (mom, dad, siblings?)
2. What were gender expectations when I was growing up?
3. Did I grow up in an urban/suburban/rural area?
4. What was my family's economic situation?
5. What were my family's most deeply held values? Where did they come from?

> 6. What were the stories told about power and respect in my family?
> 7. What were the emotional rules in my family? (What kinds of emotions were deemed acceptable versus not acceptable?)
> 8. What earned praise? What earned shaming?
> 9. Was I allowed to ask questions and challenge adults?

Based on your responses, think about the implicit and explicit messages you send about what you value—effort versus results, external measures of success versus internal ones, and so forth. Do your words match your behavior in terms of values (i.e., teamwork is important, but individual accolades are better; competition versus cooperation; "think for yourself" versus "do what I tell you to do")?

How many of your answers don't ring true for what you really value? If, for example, anger was acceptable in your childhood home but it wasn't OK to express fear or sadness, have you carried that over into your home? Do you really feel that way?

Educators can do the following exercise, adapted from Zaretta Hammond's book *Culturally Responsive Teaching and the Brain*.

> ACTIVITY: What Is My Teaching Bias?
> We all have conditioned responses and internal biases, and it can be hard to acknowledge or even understand what they are without taking the time to dig into how we were taught to teach and the context in which we work. Start by asking yourself the following questions without judgment. No answer is right or wrong: this is about gathering information so that you can respond to students in an intentional way.
>
> 1. How would I describe my teaching style? (top down, authoritative, free flowing, flexible, etc.)
> 2. What kind of teachers did I connect with and gravitate toward when I was a student?
> 3. What was my experience like as a student?
> 4. How do I identify as a person (gender, race/culture, sexuality, socioeconomic status, ability, etc.)?

5. What are my reasons for teaching? What are my most deeply held values around teaching, and what are their origins?
6. What are the stories I tell about power and respect?
7. What happens when I feel challenged?
8. What earns praise in my classroom? What earns shaming?
9. Which students do I gravitate toward the most? Which students challenge me the most, intellectually and emotionally? Which students do I have difficulty connecting with?

THE MYTH OF MULTITASKING

We are expected to multitask all the time. Job postings ask for folks who are good at it; smart phones and computer software advertise their ability to do it. We've been told that women are better at it than men because they have had more practice juggling home and work. But the fact is, our brains are not able to truly multitask—they just rapidly switch back and forth between jobs, and it happens so quickly that we don't notice it. The more we do it, the more manageable it can become, but sometimes this quick swapping leads us to thinking errors.

I have a big dog who requires walks several times a day. One day as we were out, he stopped to relieve himself in the grass alongside the street. I pulled a bag out of my pocket and bent over to clean it up just as he spotted another dog coming toward us and tugged on the leash. That slight tug led me to look up from what I was doing and slightly shift my left foot.

As I looked down the street, the toes of my foot came down on something about an inch in diameter, and I panicked, certain that I was now stepping on my dog's poop. I jumped back, nearly fell over backward, and gasped. I yanked on the leash, pulling my dog toward me in annoyance.

A second later when I looked down again, I saw that I had stepped on a branch that had fallen from a nearby tree, and I was embarrassed that I had reacted with such anger at my dog, who was just doing what he was born to do—greet other dogs with a wag of his tail.

This story illustrates how our minds connect the dots for us without having all the information. Because I had been poised to clean up my dog's mess, when I stepped on something that was slightly similar (although much harder and not in the exact same area), my brain completed the picture, initiated a fear response, and led me to act in a way I wish I hadn't.

How often have we done something similar with our children? How many times have we seen an e-mail from the school detailing some social or behavioral challenges and then, when our children get in the car and say they had a bad day, we assume we know why and react in kind? How often do we acknowledge that we don't have all the important pieces of information until we ask questions and assess the situation?

If we are aware that our brains try to help us by filling in knowledge gaps for us when we're doing more than one thing at a time, we are more likely to remember to check our assumptions. Even if we think we know what is going on, what is bothering or motivating our children, we need to step back, breathe, and remind ourselves that if our brains don't fully switch from those other tasks we were doing, we might just be making up stuff to satisfy our brain's desire to "know."

Asking questions, remaining curious, and recognizing our own limitations are key to mindful parenting and teaching and can keep us from saying or doing things that can cause conflict or erode trust.

MODELING AN EMPOWERED VIEW OF LIFE

So much of parenting and teaching is modeling. Children watch us, and many of their standard reactions to life events come about because of the way they see us react. How do you respond when things don't turn out the way you want them to: do you blame someone else, scold yourself, lament your bad luck, or rant that you "don't deserve this"? Those are all examples of disempowerment, living life as though it happens to you, feeling at the whim of fate or luck.

If youth see us as people who don't have much say over what happens in life or how we feel about it, they begin to believe and act that way, too. Watching us judge and label every experience and take things personally colors their view of the world. We definitely don't have control over everything that happens in our lives, but we do get to decide how we see those things—are they opportunities for growth or minor setbacks, or do they make us feel victimized?

When we are stuck in traffic and frustrated, screaming at other drivers or blaming our children for being five minutes late to meet us won't do anything to clear up the traffic; it only adds to the tension and annoyance everyone feels. Losing out on that job promotion you really wanted is justifiably disappointing, and it's OK to take time to process your feelings, but finding scapegoats for it gives away your power to make a change that gets you going in the direction you ultimately want to go.

> ACTIVITY: When Things Don't Go Your Way
>
> 1. Acknowledge your feelings (*I'm so angry/frustrated/nervous/sad right now.*)
> 2. Acknowledge the situation and the fact that, at least for the moment, it is unchangeable. (*We are stuck in traffic. Dinner is burned. My wallet was stolen.*)
> 3. Try to resist judging your feelings (*I shouldn't be so upset,* or *why can't I just let it go?*) or making up stories about them (*If only I hadn't . . .,* or *because of her . . .*) **This step is the hardest, and it takes a lot of practice.** Most of us barely pay attention to what we're actually feeling and leap right to justifying, or explaining, or creating scenarios in our heads about what could happen, but part of feeling empowered is letting our emotions rise and recede. If we don't fight or exaggerate our feelings with stories we create, they will peak in about ninety seconds and start to subside. Going through steps 1 and 2 can give us enough space and time to interrupt an anger or anxiety reaction.
> 4. Decide what your most important value is in regard to the situation and develop a plan to get there. (*If you will be late for an important appointment but you're stuck in traffic, can you call the person waiting for you to see if he can suggest an alternative? If dinner is burned and everyone is hungry, can you agree to have peanut butter sandwiches and play cards for a change?*)

Often, when we lead with pessimism or helplessness, or by putting ourselves at the center of the situation, we are acting out of fear or insecurity or a sense of scarcity. The best way to counteract those kinds of responses is to stop and recognize our connection to other people. If we are worried about not having enough of something to be safe, we can ask trusted friends for help. If we are fearful that a situation will get out of our control, we can stop to assess the challenges against what we know about our own strengths.

This kind of response to a difficult episode speaks volumes to young people who watch us. Showing them that it's OK to be afraid, that it's possible to work your way through it and learn from it, is a powerful lesson. Sometimes when we are stretching ourselves, we have to be willing to push through impatience, perfectionism, either/or thinking, and catastrophizing in order to find solid ground again. Letting young people see us do this can give them the courage to learn and grow, too.

Chapter Three

Trusting Relationships

There's a difference between saying "why do you think you did that?" and saying "how could you do that?" which is not a question but an accusation. Which is another way of saying, "you have forfeited your right to be understood. Shame on you."—Gregory Martin

THE BASICS: KNOWING YOURSELF AND YOUR CHILD/STUDENT

The more we develop our own self-awareness, the better our connections are with other people. It may seem obvious, but we all have different ways of seeing the world and interacting with others that influence the way we talk to people and how we feel about things. We often tend to assume that other people see things and think about things the way we do, so when we communicate with them, we do it in the ways that suit us best.

Problems can arise when other people don't quite "get it," and often that is because we have different styles and preferences.

> ACTIVITY: What's My Unique Style?
> Ask yourself the following questions and take some time to reflect on the answers. Then ask your child or students to do the same and find a time when you can share your thoughts with each other.

1. What inspires me? Where do I feel like I have influence in the world? When do I feel my intuition and trust it?
2. How are my thoughts and emotions linked?
3. Do I feel free to speak my truth? How else do I make myself known (writing, artistic expression, singing)? What happens when I am in the company of people who feel comfortable expressing themselves—am I quiet or intimidated or inspired to speak out?
4. Do I feel solid and grounded in my sense of self and who I am and how I move through the world? Am I different with different people, or am I always the same, no matter who I am with?
5. How do I best connect with others? Do I tend to make strong connections quickly, or am I cautious? Does my heart get broken easily?
6. How do I learn best? Do I prefer listening or reading, watching or doing? What happens in my head when I make mistakes?
7. How do I feel when faced with a decision? Do I tend to instantly know "in my gut" what to do, or am I more comfortable taking time to assess and reflect?

Your answers and your child's answers may change the way you decide to relate to each other and communicate. This can be a powerful way to understand why you've had miscommunications before and can really shift the dynamic.

Each of us also has an emotional style that determines how we experience the world. The six dimensions that make up our individual emotional style are:

1. **Outlook** (Are we generally optimistic or pessimistic?)
2. **Resilience** (How do we react to disappointment and mistakes?)
3. **Social intuition** (Can we "read" other people's emotions accurately?)
4. **Self-awareness** (Do we know why we do and say the things we do?)
5. **Sensitivity to context** (Do we tend to focus on one aspect of a situation, or can we see the big picture and understand the nuances?)

6. **Attention** (How able are we to focus on what we're doing and who we are with?)

These are absolutely not fixed dimensions, but knowing roughly where we are on each of these areas and where our kids are in relation to us can drastically impact the way we speak to each other and whether we are able to have empathy.

These should not be considered things to judge. We are who we are, and whether or not we have a strong sense of intuition about other people isn't good or bad, it just helps us understand a little better how we move through the world and what conditions are most conducive to our comfort and ease.

In practical terms, it is also important to understand your child's temperament. Whether your children are introverts or extroverts, whether they struggle with transitions or fly right through them without any issues, how they make decisions, and whether they are quick to emotion or more slow-burning all affect the way they see the world.

Who our children are combined with who we are determines how we interact. Understanding that I am an extrovert who loves noise and people and lots of activity around me at all times, but my child is overwhelmed by those things and needs to feel calm and centered might prevent me from planning a huge surprise party for his fifteenth birthday with all of his friends at the local video arcade. It would be fun for me, and really very terrible for him, regardless of my intent. Taking into account that we are different people who experience the world in different ways is the first step to building a relationship with intent and care.

It is our job to parent and teach children for who they are, not for who we wish they were or for who we are. We can have an impact on their outlook or resilience over time, but only if they are willing participants in that process. It is not our job to change them. It is our job to love them and help them find the most effective, most joyful way that they can navigate their lives given their unique abilities and qualities.

This is another place where the relationship between educators and families is really impactful. Listening to and learning from each other can make a huge difference in how a child fares, both at home and at school. One of you might have a tip about something that works really well to motivate a teen that the other one hadn't thought of. It's important to check with a child before sharing information that feels personal with a parent or teacher, but nothing is wrong with the two of you creating your own relationship in service to the well-being of a young person.

BARRIERS TO HEALTHY RELATIONSHIPS

When we are in healthy relationships with others, we feel safe and comfortable. Our relationship with our children is one of the most important and enduring relationships we will have in our lives, and because of the nature of it, we will see it go through many changes over the decades. Unfortunately, we often create patterns of communication and behavior with our children when they're young that don't serve any of us as they get older.

As teachers, we can fall into habits of relating to children that work for most of the youth we teach but not for all of them. Or we can become so overwhelmed with the tasks we have to manage that we let our connection to students fall by the wayside.

Whether you're a teacher or a parent, spending some time looking at barriers to healthy relationship and understanding how to plant seeds for strong connections will build new foundations that will allow us to interact in ways that feel good and are sustainable. Good relationships require our attention and feed us in really important ways by making us feel more loved and appreciated.

The first thing that keeps us from connecting with others in a healthy way is competition. So many of us grew up believing that competition is a good thing, that it's healthy. Living in a capitalist society, watching professional and collegiate sports, going to school and vying against our classmates in the spelling bee and being graded on our efforts every day, it's not surprising that we believe that competition is normal and natural and even desirable.

We compete for spots in college, jobs we want, parking spots close to the door when it's raining. We play games with our children and bet on the outcome of all sorts of things in public life, from elections to sporting events. But how does competition affect our relationships? How does it show up in ways that keep us from really being open to supporting the people we love, no matter what? How does it keep us from feeling good about ourselves? The answer lies in judgment and the messages we play again and again in our heads.

When we compete with our children by comparing them to who we were when we were children (my life was so much harder; my parents were much tougher on me; by the time I was your age, I was working and going to school all day), we are judging them. The truth is, life in the twenty-first century is very different than it was when you grew up. It is not a fair comparison, and the ultimate message is that today's youth aren't measuring up.

No amount of judgment can motivate young people to feel good about themselves, so although games with low or no stakes are fun, conversations that degrade who our children are at their core (lazy, stupid, not talented) keep them from feeling safe and connected to us. When we set up scenarios to prove to them that we are smarter/more competent/better than they are, when we say things such as, "I told you so," they feel judged, not inspired.

If what we truly want is to be in relationship with someone, we have to set aside our ego or our belief that we know better than they do how to live life. We absolutely know best how to live *our own individual* life, but being in relationship with adolescents requires creating space for them to grow into their instincts and choices.

The second barrier is power. Systems require hierarchy, and hierarchies create power dynamics. School systems, family systems, work, and sports all come with their own inherent power dynamics. But power is destructive to relationships.

When have you ever felt 100 percent safe in a position where you didn't have sovereignty over yourself and your choices? If we don't feel safe with others, we can't have a clear, healthy relationship with them. But when the relationship is designed so that someone else has power over us, we can't feel safe. It can be really difficult to imagine not having power over our children but, in general, the kinds of questions that come up are for us at home and at school center around what happens when things go wrong—who takes responsibility, who enforces the rules, who makes decisions.

If we place the emphasis instead on building strong, healthy connections, the questions can be very different and less rooted in power. We can stop worrying about who ultimately gets to be in charge and have conversations about ideal outcomes, share our vision for what success looks like, and build agreements based on mutual values. All of these things involve teens and tweens in critical thinking, problem solving, and exploring their ideas about the world and what's important, and they all lead to the development of healthy adults.

The third barrier to healthy relationships is fear. Fear is a powerful motivator, but it tends to make us move away from things rather than toward them. When we are afraid, we shut ourselves off from others, either by shrinking back and hiding, or by lashing out. Adults have a long track record of using fear to convince kids to act in certain ways, but being surrounded by messages designed to make us afraid takes a toll on our relationships.

Most of us have absorbed these messages so deeply that we have adopted the tactics of fear to use in our relationships without really thinking about it. Many of us have also created habitual responses to fear that we use in our everyday relationships, so exploring where fear shows up, how we use it, and where it makes us act in ways that we don't want to is really important if we want to learn how to be more connected to the people around us. Manipulating children by warning them of worst-case scenarios only teaches them to do one of two things: expect the worst all the time, or begin to understand that they can't believe what you say when the worst doesn't happen.

As a young parent, I remember an elder advising me to make sure that my children were tough. "The world is a harsh place, so if your kids aren't tough, they won't make it." That rang true, partially because that's the way I was raised and partially because it was easy to remember all the scary and challenging times that I'd been through myself. The human brain is wired to remember bad experiences more than good ones.

But what if, instead, we teach our children that the world is a mostly good place? That people out there will support them and help them when they need it. What if, instead of scaring our kids to toughen them up, we work on creating a world that isn't scary because people care about each other? What if we are honest with them about the fact that they will meet challenges and help them build networks of people who will support them through those challenges?

SEEDS OF HEALTHY RELATIONSHIPS

The components of a healthy relationship require courage. We have to be willing to go against much of what we've learned from the systems we have been immersed in our entire lives and stand firm in our desire to create healthy relationships. It is also important to understand that these seeds require tending and time to come to fruition. New habits and ways of being only come about after a lot of practice and effort; often, we have to go through the motions again and again before we are able to believe in and embrace what we're doing. Because so much of this goes against what we've been taught our whole lives, it will feel scary and unnatural in the beginning.

The first seed we have to plant is trust. Trust and vulnerability go hand in hand, and when I say trust, I don't only mean that sense that someone else has your back if things go sideways; I also mean that we need to practice assuming the best of others, trusting that they will act in ways that aren't intentionally harmful.

One of my favorite quotes is "trust is an outcome of honest conversation, not a prerequisite for it." That means that we have to be willing to show up and be open about who we are and what we want if we are going to gain someone's trust. But we also have to be willing to suspend judgment and assume good intent, not begin with suspicion or being guarded.

As parents, we often tell our children that they have to earn our trust, but the irony of that is that until we take a little leap of faith and give them opportunities to make their own choices, they can't do that. In other words, we have to trust them at least a little first if they are going to prove to us that they're ready for that.

A WORD ABOUT PRIVACY

As children get older, they begin to crave more privacy, which can feel threatening to parents and teachers. We often begin to wonder what the other person is hiding from us. We get suspicious.

Privacy	Secrecy
Safe place to be myself, agency	Invokes power over, hiding, done out of fear
Strengthens relationships with others	Erodes relationships
Liberating, relaxing	Stressful, hard to maintain

Bell hooks writes about the distinction between privacy and secrecy, and her explanation is helpful here.

Offering children privacy as they work out who they are, what is important to them, and how they want to show up in the world builds trust and connections. Even if you're afraid that they are hiding something, if you focus on the strength of the relationship, because of the stress of maintaining a lie, other people will often choose to "come clean," but only if they believe they can trust you to treat them with care and compassion.

Unless you have reason to believe that children are likely to harm themselves or someone else, letting them have a safe place to be themselves—a journal or a friendship that doesn't involve you—might feel scary, but is ultimately a sign that you trust them to know what's right for them.

The second seed is cooperation. Cooperation is the flip side of competition, and although we are often encouraged to cooperate with others, we are generally still "graded" individually by teachers or parents or bosses. It can be hard to both collaborate with someone and know that you are ultimately in competition with them, but building strong communities and families comes when we can find ways to truly work together to achieve an outcome.

There is a way to align with others even as we recognize that we bring different things to the table and that those things are equally valuable. Learning to cocreate goals and navigate challenges in true partnership is difficult, but the benefit to feeling as though you are an integral part of something bigger than yourself is immense. As a parent, that requires inviting your children into the conversations about the things that are important to them. It also means asking them to step up and help others in the family to show their willingness to plant this seed.

As a teacher, it means understanding who your students are, how they learn, and what is important to them. It means listening to them when they tell you what they find inspiring or challenging, and working with them to try different ways of learning the material you most want to teach them. It means offering them opportunities to speak up and helping them listen better.

The final seed is reciprocity. Reciprocity refers to the flow of energy and gifts between two people. So often, we don't see ourselves as true equals with others we are in relationship with, either because we're in competition, because a power differential exists, or because we don't feel secure in our own gifts and talents and worth. But when we are connected to people with whom we give and receive freely, without keeping score or weighing one set of attributes against another, we can feel secure and safe and cared for.

Practicing reciprocity is difficult, especially if others are not willing to give up their ideas about competition and power and fear, but when we find people who are, it is truly magic. When we know that our children are interested in us as human beings and want us to be well and happy as much as we want that for them, we are on the road to a loving, lasting connection.

All partners in a relationship deserve to have their needs met, and as long as we plant these seeds and continue to practice honesty, communication even when it hurts, and devotion to the connection we have, we can meet each other's needs. Relationships don't grow when one person benefits more than the other. That doesn't mean that things will always be equal, but it should mean that everyone is invested in the work.

SHAME AND EMPATHY

Shame shuts down pathways to learning in the brain. It is also a destructive emotion that isolates us from other people. Dr. Brené Brown, a researcher at the University of Houston, writes about shame and guilt and defines the difference between them as simple but important. Guilt comes about when we acknowledge that we have made a mistake. Shame is what happens to us when we personalize that mistake and let it define us. It is the difference between saying "I did a bad thing" and "I am a bad person."

Shame tells us that we are damaged goods and we have no way back. Guilt makes us reflect on our actions and think about how to atone for them or learn from them, but it doesn't doom us forever. This is why the language we use with our children is so critical. It is their job to make mistakes because that is how human beings learn best, but if we teach them that making mistakes can turn them into horrible people, they will feel hopeless.

Calling children out for lying is holding them responsible for one bad act. Calling them a liar means that we are defining them in that way. We have branded them a certain type of person, rather than acknowledging that they lied. If we do that often enough, children internalize those messages and feel almost obligated to live out that prophecy.

As a child, I was often shamed by my parents because they had learned it was an effective tactic to keep me in line and ensure that I acted in a certain way. I learned that the most important thing to do was the "right" thing, but what I didn't learn was how to determine what the "right" thing was every single time. I was afraid to try things because I was afraid to make a mistake and be shamed for it.

Shame is certainly effective at changing short-term behavior, but only because people want to avoid being shamed, not because it changes what they value. It's important to know this because someone who is acting in a certain way to avoid punishment or shame eventually will find a way to stop being in relationship with you. Over time, they stop engaging with you or find ways to hide their "shameful" behaviors from you. I got really good at lying to my parents.

If we really want to be in relationships with our children that are honest and open and be able to help them learn from their mistakes, shame is the wrong way to go about it. Shame teaches children that they *are* their mistakes, and their brains shut down the learning pathways. If children are afraid to take risks and try things, they can't learn as well, and if they're overwhelmed with emotion, they're not processing language or using their PFC.

Empathy Is the Opposite of Shame

Having empathy for our children means being able to walk a mile in their shoes and see things from their perspective. Just because we can have empathy for them does not mean that we excuse their behavior. I can recall doing some pretty stupid things when I was a teenager, and I am so relieved that none of them are seen as the entire story of who I am and what I could become. Remembering this when my children mess up helps me to have kindness in my heart for them, even when I am angry or frustrated or fearful of the consequences of their actions.

Finding empathy is the beginning of separating my reactions from my children's behavior. Once I do that, I can talk to them without an agenda other than working on solutions to the mess they find themselves in. When I set aside my emotions, I can ask, "Why do you think you did that?," and they can begin to develop self-awareness. They can start to understand how they found themselves in this situation and assess whether they were acting according to their values (who they really are) at the time.

Even if your teens can't answer the question "Why do you think you did that?," the simple act of asking it signals your curiosity about them and gives them the chance to practice examining the choices they make. If that is your first reaction, instead of, "What is wrong with you?," or "That was so stupid!," it allows them the space to reflect on the behavior without getting defensive or feeling bad about themselves.

Often, the first words we speak are words we heard when our parents or teachers were upset with us. It's worth taking a moment to hear them in your head and remember how they made you feel as a young person. And it's important to then take another moment to decide what your objective is—to make others feel stupid, or to help them learn from the situation. You may well have "told them so," but saying that doesn't do anything except signal that you feel superior. Remember, the decisions they make are fueled by emotion and an immature brain.

ALTERNATIVES TO SHAME AND BLAME

DO remember how important it is for children to be held in positive regard by their loved ones. Feeling like they belong is basic survival to a teen. Being mocked or criticized—especially in front of others—often feels incredibly painful and frightening.

DON'T try to motivate them by embarrassing them. It will only mean they learn you can't be trusted to support them emotionally.

DO remember that we learn best in relationship.

DON'T make it personal. Teens are very self-critical, and the worse they feel about themselves, the more self-absorbed they become. This can start a spiral that lands them in isolation or frustration from which they can't see a way out.

DO acknowledge their positive attributes. Focusing on what they are doing well helps them think about how they can contribute positively and helps reinforce the message that you want to see them succeed.

DON'T have all the answers. Part of helping teens means letting them know that we think they are capable of coming up with solutions.

DO ask lots of questions. What are they struggling with? Where could they use more support?

Chapter 3
TRUST

Trust is an outcome of honest conversation, not a prerequisite for it.

We all know that trust is an important part of good relationships, but we don't always know how to go about creating it. One of the first things that has to be present for there to be trust is a feeling of safety. If I know that I can say what I truly feel without being attacked or mocked for it, I am much more likely to be honest, and the more honest I am, the more likely others will be honest as well.

Another important part of trust involves knowing that the other person or people are truly curious about where I'm coming from. When we are curious about our children, we let them know that their thoughts and feelings and values are important to us. Asking lots of questions is a great way to get to know what makes our children tick. What do they value most? Why do they choose to do or say some of the things they do? How do they see the world and their place in it? These kinds of questions validate our children's right to have an opinion, even if it's different from ours, and it gives them an opportunity to identify what they want from life and practice speaking up about it.

It is important for adolescents to have opportunities to cocreate their values and identities with trusted, caring adults. Human beings need to feel as though they are in relationship with others who acknowledge their reality and their right to see things in a certain way. Even if we can't understand why our children feel a particular way, we can let them know that they have a right to their emotions and that we are available to them for processing and healing.

Western cultural values often center on individuality and independence, but the truth is, none of us is truly independent. Helping our children develop a system for deciding whom to trust will prove valuable to them for the rest of their lives.

When my oldest daughter was struggling with something as a high-school student, she came to me and said she wished she knew who to talk to who could help her. I gave her a piece of advice that has worked for me: tell the people who have earned the right to hear your most difficult moments; the people who have shown you they won't use your fear and vulnerability to their own advantage, either by gossiping about it, making fun of you, or using it against you later. Talk to someone who shows you through their behavior that they care about you, someone who doesn't judge you for feeling the way you feel, who asks how they can help and then follows through with support.

ACTIVITY: Building Trust

The following exercise was created by Kim Bogucki, founder of the IF Project, in an attempt to build bridges between prison inmates and police officers—two communities that historically don't trust each other at all. Sit down with your children when you have some time and ask them to answer these three questions—either orally or written. You answer the same questions about them and see if it spurs conversation or insights about each other.

- What is one belief or perception I have about you?
- What is one thing you don't know about me?
- What would make our interaction easier for me?

It may seem simple, but often the answers to the first two questions are pretty surprising. The last question offers both of you the chance to define your own boundaries and be creative about how to maintain and strengthen your relationship.

As adults, we often focus on how trust is violated, and although that is part of being in relationship, it often happens as a result of mistakes. When young persons you trusted mess up somehow, take a minute to think about whether their act was personal or not. Lying about you to another person, deliberately attempting to hurt you, or violating a confidence are all behaviors that break interpersonal trust and require repair.

Violating curfew, trying to cover up a misstep, and going around the rules to get something they want are behaviors that break rules, and on some level violate trust, but they aren't personal acts that require personal repair. That doesn't mean they don't deserve discussion, but more often than not they indicate a difference in values or a momentary lapse of judgment. When we can discern which kinds of things to take personally, we can often defuse potentially emotional situations and work to have more productive conversations with young people.

Being able to talk about issues that arise strengthens trust between two people. Treating every slight as though it has the same weight and issuing ultimatums only leads to fear and mistrust. Just like we feel powerless when our children slam the door and refuse to talk to us, they feel powerless when we hand out punishments or consequences without any discussion or consideration for their perspective.

MAKING MISTAKES

We know that children this age make decisions mostly based on emotions, even if they try to rationalize those choices to themselves or others. The truth is, we all sometimes make emotional decisions and use logic to justify our choices without even realizing it.

When your teens or tweens make a decision for some reason known only to them (I blew my entire allowance on that music download because I'm the only one who doesn't know all the words to those songs, and I need to fit in or I'll feel like a loser), you will not be able to talk them out of the underlying emotions (embarrassment, fear, anxiety). The best you can do is acknowledge the emotion (fitting in is really important, and being socially isolated is scary) and help them become aware of the driving factor behind the choice.

Again, it is important that we not mock or judge children for the underlying issue. It may seem as though the best thing to say is "don't pay any attention to what other kids think of you," but their reality is such that they feel they have to. Remember, belonging is not just some nicety in the adolescent world—it is survival. Even if we can't sympathize with it, we can acknowledge that it exists.

Once children have had some practice getting to the meat of their emotions, help them define some of their other values (saving money for that summer trip, helping pay for their phone bill to stay connected to friends) and strategize about ways to achieve the same goal (learning the words to the songs) without spending all their money. Bringing the "why" out into the light helps them think about whether the choice was worth the outcome. If they were motivated by knowing the words but ended up feeling angry and frustrated that they didn't have any money left to go to the movies with friends on Friday night, that's important information.

The trick here is to avoid injecting your personal values into the conversations. Remember, you will not talk them out of their feelings, and if you try, the message they will likely get is that their feelings are somehow "wrong." Ultimately, if this happens enough, your children won't talk to you about their feelings anymore, and because children are walking warehouses of emotion for about ten years, that doesn't leave much for the two of you to talk about.

One goal of this particular phase of development is to learn to make good choices, but we have to make them according to our own beliefs and value systems. The best (and likely most frustrating) thing you can do is help teens identify their goals and determine whether their actions are in line with those goals. Practice is key.

> PARENTING TIP: Shorthand for Tweens and Teens
> When my oldest daughter was in the sixth grade, we lived about forty-five minutes' drive from her school. This gave us plenty of time both to prepare for and debrief from her days in middle school. For the first twenty minutes of the drive home, several other girls were in our carpool, and I loved listening to them chat about classwork and teachers and social dynamics. From time to time, after everyone else had been dropped off, my daughter would sigh and prepare to complain about something that was bothering her.
> At first, my instinct was to home in on the "problem" and offer solutions. I assumed that she was telling me because she wanted my help, and often, I interrupted to tell a story from my childhood that I thought was similar. Not surprisingly, she often got frustrated with me, both for interrupting and for making it about me. Pretty soon, I figured out that if I kept doing this, she would stop talking to me about anything important.
> I assumed that she was telling me these things because she trusted me, and she probably was, but she was shutting down and getting angry because I wasn't returning that level of trust. By interrupting and giving her advice, I was letting her know that I didn't trust her to handle the situation herself or think creatively about it. I was giving her the answer to make myself feel better.
> If I gave her the solution, I didn't have to see her struggle any longer. Once I realized that I was making it all about me, I created a shorthand for us. Whenever she indicated that she needed to talk about something important, I asked, "What do you need from me right now? Is this venting, do you want my opinion, or are you asking for my advice?"
> More often than not, she was simply venting in a safe space without teachers or friends to overhear. Once she said so, I could relax and just listen. Nothing more was required of me than to be a friendly ear. I didn't get caught up in emotion or rush to imagine how to fix anything. She just needed to release her frustrations and move on.

> From time to time, as she wound down, she changed her mind and asked for my opinion on the situation. Very occasionally, she asked for my advice.
>
> The most important part of all of this was that it gave her control over the interaction and let me know what role I was playing. Often as she talked, she came up with her own solution, and generally it was something I never would have thought of. When she was simply venting, I was able to reinforce the message that sometimes what we really need is to let go of the things we can't control and move on. But most important, it allowed us to have boundaries around our relationship and reminded her that I am a safe place to land when she feels unhappy.

DEVELOPMENTAL RELATIONSHIP THEORY

When our children are little, it doesn't take long to realize that we can't keep them safe and healthy all by ourselves. We have to enlist other trusted folks to help us out: grandparents, babysitters, teachers—people who make sure they don't dash out into the street or eat slugs or fall off the bed. Other people teach them things we can't—social skills, multiplication tables, how to play kickball—even if we are still there, helping them nearly every step of the way.

When our children hit the middle- and high-school years, we are told that the best thing we can do is back off and let them become independent and self-sufficient. If we don't, we're accused of being overprotective or "helicopter parents." Frustratingly, during this time, it's often hard for us to know who these other people are that our kids are learning from. Curriculum night doesn't establish trusting relationships with teachers. Meeting the coaches once or twice doesn't really show us who they are. And often, our kids make friends with new children whose families we don't know. So, what's a parent to do?

It doesn't help that many teens have a nasty habit of trying to convince us that they don't need anyone's help—that they're just little adults, and they'll be fine, and if they do need something, they'll ask their friends. But they aren't little adults, and now we're not worried about them eating slugs, we're worried about them taking drugs or skipping class. And because we're encouraged to back off and let them be more independent, we often don't know that things have gone sideways until they're five assignments behind in math or about to be suspended. Regardless of how badly children this age want to be seen as grown up and capable, they don't have the life experience or brain development to handle really complex situations on their own, so it's important that we help them develop dynamic, progressive relationships with adults who support, challenge, and care for them in different ways. We can't just put them in a time-out and hope to change their behavior.

We have to help them learn to make educated decisions and take responsibility for their choices, but it doesn't happen overnight. We can't just expect them to go from riding a tricycle to a two-wheeler in one fell swoop. They need training wheels to hold them up when we can't be there so that they can get used to the road, and those training wheels often take the form of other adults who will support and push our children to grow.

No matter how well we think we know our children, we don't know every facet of their personality. I've been at parent-teacher conferences where I'm convinced that we aren't talking about the same person because my child is described as "quiet, compliant, and helpful." Huh? Who? The fact is, our teens *need* to be different to different people. It's vital that they have lots of opportunities to test out ways of being and bump up against different rules and situations. That's life.

The connections our teens have with adults other than parents have an incredible impact on their ability to navigate the world with confidence and support, and the fact is, they are often more likely to listen to those folks than they are to us once they hit the adolescent years. So how do we help them find the right adults?

When my oldest daughter was sixteen, she got a job at a local bakery. Despite the myriad attempts I had made to teach her the family recipes I love so much over the years, she never cared. She said cooking and baking weren't her "thing." But then, she came home from this new job buzzing with energy, telling us over dinner that she spent her day making hundreds of cookies and hand pies and "learned so much!"

It was hard not to be irritated, but she learned a lot more about collaboration and cooperation and deferring to someone with expertise at that job than she ever would have from me, partially because she was being guided gently by someone who didn't already have a personal relationship with her. When she was corrected, she was much less likely to take it personally, and she paid much closer attention. The stakes were different.

Bosses and mentors, teachers and coaches, aunts and religious leaders and grandparents are all examples of people who see our children differently than we do and expect different things from them. And they're all incredibly important pieces of the puzzle. These relationships have the potential to gradually build our children's confidence and emotional intelligence and networks. According to the Search Institute, these kinds of connections build what's known as developmental relationships.

Five crucial elements of relationships teens need in order to thrive are:

1. **Caring** (Who in this teen's life is dependable, warm, offers encouragement, listens to the teen, and helps build her confidence?)
2. **Growth** (Who sees this teen's potential, holds him accountable for his choices, and helps him reflect on his mistakes and define areas for improvement?)
3. **Support** (Who guides her through systems shey encountes, empowers her to find her own path, advocates for her, and helps her stay on track?)
4. **Shares Power** (Who respects this teen, includes him in important decisions, collaborates with him, and gives him opportunities to lead?)
5. **Expands Possibilities** (Who inspires this teen to dream, exposes her to new ideas, and connects her to other people who can inform and assist her?)

The beauty of this is that you don't have to be all of those things to your teens, and it's likely that they already have some folks in their lives who are filling these requirements. It is important, however, to know that they do have trusted connections with people who do these things because that is how they become secure enough in their abilities and skills to venture into the world one day and spread their wings.

Being intentional about helping young people find adults who will fill those shoes for them can be incredibly impactful. Sit down with your child or your class of students and ask them to brainstorm who in their life does any of these things for them? There will be gaps, for sure, but knowing where they are can help identify areas that might be vital to their development. It may spur them to start a conversation with a school staff member or start texting an uncle regularly. And for you as a parent, it can give you some peace of mind that your child is in good hands.

COMMUNICATION

Building trusting relationships requires effective communication techniques. Unfortunately, we are susceptible to relying on patterns of communication that don't always work as our children get older. And the older they get, the better they get at recognizing when we're distracted, disconnected, and not being totally honest with them.

> ACTIVITY: Am I Being Heard?
> Think about an experience you have had when you were misunderstood, and it caused a problem. Then think about a time when you had a conversation with someone, and you really felt seen and heard.
>
> - How do you know which is which? Describe the experience including nonverbal communication.
> - How did the two scenarios feel different?
> - Are there people in your life you know will almost always truly hear you?
> - Can you think of a time when you weren't fully present for a conversation with a child, and it caused conflict and misunderstanding?
> - How can you ask to be heard the next time you need it?

As the parent or adult in charge, your number one resource in times of high emotion is your ability to find a place of calm. Taking a minute to check your emotional temperature, finding a way to be present, and settling your mind and body will not only keep you from escalating the situation, but it can prevent misunderstandings and, because we feed off of each other's energy, it will help your children regulate their emotional response as well.

We learn patterns of communication from our family of origin and, in turn, we teach them to our children. If your children have suffered trauma, it is important to recognize that shouting, an angry look on your face, or turning away can cause them to react more forcefully than they might have otherwise. We need to not only be clear with ourselves what we hope to gain from an interaction with our children, but we need to explain it to them in a way that they understand as well.

Further, if you have a history of trauma, it's good to take a minute when you're feeling emotional and acknowledge that. Often, our habitual responses—physical and verbal—happen so quickly that they can seem overwhelming and, as the adults in the room, we can set a tone for the interaction that is way off base. It is entirely possible that your trauma history leads you to interact with a teen who reminds you of yourself or someone in your past in a way that is harmful for both of you. Taking the time to calm your body and mind and get present with who you are right now and who this child is can prevent conflict.

It is also vital that you understand your own communication preference and your child's. We tend to communicate with others in the way that we want to be communicated with, but that's not always effective. I tend to struggle to process complex ideas just by listening, so I doodle or make notes or e-mail people when I want to "talk." Other people don't process by reading or visual cues, and they prefer to hear (these are people who love audiobooks, whereas I can't focus for more than about two minutes on an audiobook before my mind starts to wander). Still others need to be physically moving while they're processing information, so they prefer to communicate while going for a walk or doing a puzzle or building something.

When I was first married, my husband and I struggled to communicate about things that needed to get done outside of work. We both worked full-time, and often, one of us had to remind the other one to do something—call the insurance company on a lunch break or feed the cat. I chose to leave him notes—bright squares on the fridge or his car windshield as a prompt. He left me voice mail messages. It was a disaster.

I am a visual processor, so it made sense to me to leave Post-its everywhere. He is an auditory processor, so in his mind, voice mails were the only way to go. Fortunately, we were able to laugh at how ineffective the other person was—"you forget everything I tell you do to"—instead of getting angry. But once we figured out the issue, everything changed. I started leaving him voice mails, and he started texting me or leaving me notes. It was amazing how quickly that turned everything around for us.

Knowing how your child processes information best can help you design a way to communicate that works for both of you and might mean the difference between a really productive talk and one rife with misunderstandings and confusion. It can also mean that the dishwasher gets emptied after school if you ask in the right way.

NONVIOLENT COMMUNICATION

Nonviolent communication recognizes that your needs might be different from mine. It's our job as adults to both identify and acknowledge our needs in any situation (especially when there is conflict) *and* be curious about our children's needs. When we approach them with the understanding that all communication is an attempt to have our needs met, we can focus the conversation on what is most important.

Typically, a power differential exists between parents or teachers and children, which can change the quality of our interactions. When someone feels desperate to have their needs met, they tend to express that in ways that are less than ideal. If they already feel disempowered, they can think they need to come in forcefully or spend a lot of time justifying or defending their position. Often, demands come as a result of desperation; and remember, when we are hungry, stressed, overtired (and a teenager), desperation can feel really overwhelming.

If we can try to get to the root of the issue, we can begin to work to solve the need. Acknowledging the power differential is key if teens come to you already defensive. Once you feel as though you have a handle on what they're really seeking, you can address the way they asked. The primary goal is to calm the biological response, address the need, and then create an environment where learning can take place.

The other effect this approach has is to remind our children that we are committed to helping them find ways to have their needs met. The message that we care about them and want to be part of the solution is powerful, and it places their well-being above our need to be spoken to in a particular way. That creates secure attachment and a strong trust.

If we respond to demands with resistance or demands of our own, we risk damaging the relationship by escalating the situation. It can help to pretend that your children are traveling in a foreign land and they are lost and seeking help. If you focus less on the actual words and more on what is beneath them, it's possible to try to clarify what they are looking for.

And because parents and teachers are people, it's possible that our patterns of communication make it hard for us to engage in conversations like this with our teens.

ACTIVITY: My Patterns of Communication

Take a few minutes to reflect on the questions below to get a sense of how you communicate with others most of the time. In general,

- Do I speak easily and freely and feel as though I am clear?
- Do I tend to leave space for others to speak?
- Am I most comfortable listening or speaking?

With regard to conflict, there are four basic types of relating. Take a few minutes to identify your dominant tendency:

1. Conflict avoidance—comes from fear of loss of connection or safety. Characterized by self-doubt, mistrust, confusion.
2. Competitive confrontation—hyper-focused on my own needs being met. Characterized by blaming, judging, demanding, coercing, threatening.
3. Passivity—comes from a lack of valuing my own needs. Characterized by resentment, decreased connection, inability to discern my own needs over time.
4. Passive-aggression—comes from trying to meet my own needs but not those of others. Characterized by helplessness, contempt, mistrust.

The clearer we are about our intentions, the more we can communicate our needs to the other person. The clearer we are about our communication style, the more aware we are of how we might be received by the other person. One really good question to ask when someone says something that hurts us is, "How did you think I would hear that?" That's also a good question to ask when we're considering what we will say back. How do you want the other person to hear it?

Again, it's vital to remember that so often we are in positions of power over our children, meaning that getting our needs met might look a lot different for us than it does for our them. For example, if we both have the same need, which is to feel safe and be heard, it's entirely possible that what that means to me is very different than what it means to you. I might feel safest if I'm not challenged or disagreed with, and you might only feel safe if you are allowed to speak freely and disagree.

Understanding exactly what it looks like to have my needs met and your needs met can often make an enormous difference in the way we communicate and solve an issue. Taking the step to have that conversation can be a great way to enlighten both of you and might open up new avenues of understanding.

ACTIVITY: Highs and Lows

You can do this activity as a family from time to time. It's fairly low key, and as long as everyone sticks to the guidelines, it is simple and gives each family member an opportunity to share something the others might not have known otherwise. Do it in the car on the way to school, or sitting around the dinner table on Sunday night. Take turns sharing the low points of the past week with your family as well as the high points. They can be anything from tripping over the curb in public and feeling foolish to a painful breakup. Make sure everyone has a chance to talk uninterrupted, and lay down the ground rules:

1. Don't take anything personally. *This isn't about you (even if your son says his lowest moment of the last week was the fight you two had on Tuesday). This is time for everyone to share an experience that laid them low. That's all. Not taking anything personally will mean everyone gets to be as honest as possible.*
2. Don't make it personal. *Your low point has to be about you. Calling someone out for something they said or did isn't fair—especially if it happened days ago. Absolutely express that your low point was when you were sad that there was an argument about laundry, but don't say it was "when Markus left his dirty clothes on the floor for everyone to trip over."*
3. No "fixing." *It is incredibly tempting to offer advice when someone talks about being upset or sad, but now is not the time. This exercise is about sharing experiences and getting perspective on the lives of our loved ones. If someone wants advice, he can indicate that after you're finished, but there should be no interruptions when someone else is talking.*

4. No judgment. *It is also tempting to compare our low points to others' (mine was worse than yours) or somehow express that we think someone else is overreacting. It is not helpful to judge how anyone else reacts emotionally to difficult situations. What might be hard for someone else doesn't faze you at all, and that's OK, but don't belittle someone else's highs or lows just because you would have acted differently. You're not trying to convince her to be like you. The purpose of this exercise is to understand her a little more.*
5. End with the highs. *Doing it this way reminds us that we can choose how we see the world every single day. Leaving with the highs fresh in our mind is more likely to give us a boost that will last for a while.*

Chapter Four

Compassion

It is sometimes hard to have compassion for our teens, especially when we are fearful for their safety or afraid that we messed up somewhere along the way and turned them into horrible people. So often, we assume that we know what motivates them (greed, narcissism, selfishness, simply not thinking), and we react accordingly, but compassion is necessary for good, strong relationships. Being willing to spend time in the other person's shoes and proactively work to make things better is important for connection.

Often, what we are reacting to when it comes to our children is the remembrance of what we were like as teens. Remaining curious about our children without judgment is the first step toward developing compassion for them, which means stopping short of assuming that we know what they're all about. It takes practice, but it's worth the effort.

Positive emotions literally change our approach to life. When we feel calm and happy and optimistic, we are more flexible, more able to attune to our surroundings, more creative, and more resourceful. Positive emotions alter our biochemistry by producing oxytocin, a hormone that prompts us to connect with others around us; activating our vagus nerve, which calms us and helps regulate our emotions and affects our brain by modulating the activity in the amygdala and making us more likely to trust others.

All of this means that when we react to others with compassion instead of anger or frustration, we are changing their approach to the situation. Even if we feel anger or frustration, shifting to compassion can change the entire outcome of our interaction with them, and it costs us nothing. We are still able to address any issues and correct problems, but now we're doing it with flexibility, creativity, and resourcefulness.

Where there is bad behavior, there is pain.

When one of my daughters was in elementary school, she was easily overwhelmed by certain situations with lots of sensory input. She hated the volume in a movie theater; she was paralyzed by the sights and sounds and smells and people offering food samples at Costco. She was very particular about the kind of clothes she would wear, hated tags, and was a little consumed with making things "even."

Over the years, she taught herself ways to accommodate or avoid things that made her agitated, and when she started middle school, she was adept at challenging herself to endure some difficult situations in order to practice desensitizing herself. She was terribly susceptible to motion sickness and struggled with transitions for many years—especially the first few weeks of summer and the first few weeks of a new school year.

One year when she was in elementary school, we decided to surprise the children with a trip over mid-winter break. We live in a fairly dark, rainy climate and planned a trip to find some sun. My husband and I orchestrated everything without any suspicion until the night before we left when we gave them each a packing list complete with shorts and swimsuits. They were thrilled.

I didn't stop to consider what this would be like for our youngest, but by the third day of the trip, she was on edge. She had spent two full days getting herself from the beach to the pool, lying in the sunshine reading, and going for walks on the beach, but now it was Day Three.

My husband and our oldest daughter got up for a sunrise walk on the beach, and the youngest and I lounged in bed and promised to meet them in a bit. We eventually made our way into our swimsuits, then L complained that she couldn't get her hair to lie down the way she wanted and dropped her hairbrush on the tile floor. I rolled my eyes, dropped the beach bag I was holding, and wet a washcloth thoroughly to help plaster down her hair.

"As soon as it dries, it's gonna stick up all over again!," she yelled. I shushed her, worried that she would wake our hotel neighbors. She stomped her foot and glared at me.

Next, she complained that the strings on her swimsuit bottoms made "uncomfortable lumps" beneath her shorts, and she tugged and fussed and picked at it while enormous tears formed in her eyes. I was ready to go, and I needed coffee. She was being ridiculous. I told her to "figure it out."

When she couldn't get her flip flops to go on smoothly, she caught one of them in her toes and flung it across the room, where it smacked into the picture hanging above the bed. I was furious and pretty close to grabbing her by the arm as I shushed her again, warning her not to wake up anyone else.

"I DON'T CARE ABOUT THE NEIGHBORS!," she shouted, and I found myself at a crossroads. Mentally cataloging the morning's catastrophes—from the itchy, sandy shoes to her hair sticking up, to sunburned shoulders and lumpy bikini bottoms, I suddenly stopped.

Where there is bad behavior, there is pain.

This had all the earmarks of a classic transition meltdown. Each of those little, petty things normally would not phase her. She wasn't trying to be difficult; she was hurting. I set down the bag and joined her on the bed, where she lay face down, sobbing with spine-shaking gulps.

"I think that this might be what it looks like to be uncomfortable in your own skin. Do you think so?" I kissed the top of her head as she nodded emphatically.

"I – I – I don't know what to doooooo," she wailed pathetically, and my heart broke a little. She was asking for help the only way she knew how.

"I'm so sorry we sprang this trip on you, and I know you're doing your best to enjoy it. Do you think we can find a way to help you settle in a bit and start to feel more in control of things?" I led her through some deep breathing exercises and a quick guided meditation. When she was calm, we sat and talked about what she wanted to be in charge of.

She wasn't punished for her behavior. Instead, I taught her how to begin to recognize when she feels out of control, and we brainstormed ways for her to let someone know that she needs help before it gets too big. By the time we were finished, she felt like I was her ally and she knew how important she was to me. And I learned that we can't just expect our children to recognize when they're struggling and how to communicate that to us: we have to teach them that. And if we don't teach them that when they're young, they learn that bad behavior is a way to get attention from someone, even if it's an unpleasant kind of attention. Because when you're hurting, being alone is sometimes worse than being in trouble.

> **ACTIVITY: Ask Yourself First**
> One way to begin thinking about how to relate to your child with compassion is to define what you need when you're struggling. It sounds simple, but we don't often react to our children the same way we'd like to be treated when we are upset. Try to remember a time when you were really challenged by something emotionally and answer these questions:
>
> - What do I need to hear when I'm struggling? *Do you need to hear that it's not your fault? That someone loves me anyway? Do I need a reminder that I'm not alone?*
> - When I pour out my heart to someone, what do I want them to do most? *You might think you want them to "fix" it, but maybe what you want is a hug, or just someone to sit with you while you grieve.*

Ask your children what they want most when they're struggling. We don't all want the same thing, and it's important that we meet people where they are and give them a chance to define their boundaries.

The Opposite of What You Know Is Also True

One lesson I share with children in the SELF Project curriculum is just as applicable for parents. During a TED talk, Derek Sivers told a story about traveling in Japan. He was looking for a particular place and stopped someone to ask for the address. The person he asked gave him the name of a block in the city, but that confused him. He tried to clarify and asked for the name of the street. The man answered, "The streets don't have names. Streets are simply the empty space between blocks. The blocks have names."

Derek was confounded. Clearly, there was a language barrier. He tried again, and the man asked, "What is the name of the block you live on?"

Derek replied, "The blocks don't have names. The streets have names. The blocks are simply the empty spaces between streets."

In some villages in parts of Asia, local health practitioners are paid on a daily basis by the people in the village. They come by each morning to collect coins from a box placed outside for that purpose. If they happen upon a box that is empty, they know that someone inside is sick and in need of their services. In those villages, the practitioners are only paid if everyone in their care is healthy. They believe that this is the best way to ensure that everyone stays healthy, or at least does their best to prevent illness.

It is impossible for our brains to hold two opposing ideas simultaneously. Consider this famous drawing of an old lady/young lady by W. E. Hill:

Some people will immediately see an old woman wearing a bonnet on, chin tucked into her collar. Others will see a young woman with her head turned away in profile, only the tip of her nose and her eyelash visible.

We can't see both the older woman and the young woman at the same time, but our brains can flip back and forth between the two. Consider how, when we're caught up in our own ideas and stories about what our children are doing, we are literally unable to consider

Figure 4.1.   My wife and my mother-in-law. *W. E. Hill, 1915*

another option. But if we can work on the ability to let go of our assumptions and remember that the opposite of what we "know" is also true (from a different perspective), we can begin to find compassion and understanding.

In general, we tend to have a lot in common with our children or students, but it is possible that the context in which they experience life is very different from our experience. If your child is a first-generation American immigrant, her experience is very different from yours. If you are a teacher at a school with a fairly affluent student body but one of your students lives in poverty, his day-to-day reality is likely something you can't truly relate to.

In myriad ways you can see the world through one lens that is nearly the opposite of the way a young person sees it. And it costs you nothing to ask about her experience and share yours. This is how we build empathy and compassion for one another.

BARRIERS TO KINDNESS

Some parenting experts will tell you that parenting isn't about being friends with your children. Many of us were parented with a "tough love" philosophy that held us accountable for everything and worked to build us into strong, independent adults who could handle all sorts of difficult situations alone. The truth is, human beings are rarely completely on their own, though. And although we may not necessarily strive to be friends with our children, that doesn't mean we can't be kind.

At work, we are expected to collaborate and help one another. At home, if we live with other people, we need to know how to cooperate and support each other's needs. In our marriages and committed relationships, we don't always act as two separate, independent adults; we are interdependent. Even as it is important to be able and willing to be responsible for our actions and choices, it is equally as important to know our personal limitations and be able to find people we can rely on when we need it most.

It is tempting to think that once children reach high school, they need to practice cleaning up all of their own messes. Many teachers and school administrators advise parents of teens to back off and let them suffer in order to learn. It is important for teens to develop resilience and responsibility, but that doesn't mean we can't offer emotional support and kindness when they make mistakes. And it doesn't mean that they need to "suffer."

Sometimes it is hard to watch our children struggle, and I've been guilty of pretending that I'm indifferent to their suffering just so they won't be tempted to rely on me too much, but I'm not sure that ultimately sends the message I want to send. I hope that my children will come to me for emotional support; and if they really find themselves in trouble, I hope they know adults in their lives who can help them brainstorm solutions. If they're only asking their peers for help, they're counting on people without wisdom and life experience, and if they're not asking for help at all, they're taking on too much and will eventually burn out.

When our children feel low or trapped, it is never wrong to show them kindness, regardless of how they got there. It is easy to fall prey to some of these myths about kindness, but I hope you examine them and think about whether they're true in your life and relationships.

- *I can't help you.* Sometimes we feel as though being kind to someone means giving them an out or coming up with a solution for their problem. But in all honesty, we always have kindness to offer, and kindness is always helpful. It's amazing how far a hug or a smile or a simple acknowledgment of how hard a situation is goes toward letting children know we love and support them.
- *I'll look weak.* When we are angry with our children (especially if they've done what we cautioned them against and ended up where we knew they would), it's tempting to stick to our guns and either punish them or say, "I told you so." We often think we will look as though we're caving in if we commiserate, but that's not true. It is possible to empathize ("Ouch, that must have hurt," or "I'm sorry you feel that way right now") and still uphold family rules or enforce consequences.
- *I'll be taken advantage of.* This is a variation of number two. But if you show kindness and still enforce the rules, you will have demonstrated to your children that you care for them and that they are responsible for their choices. This is a powerful example of unconditional love, and there's nothing to take advantage of in that scenario.
- *I'm too angry/sad to be nice right now.* This one is tricky, but as the adult in the relationship, it's important to model this behavior. Being overwhelmed with emotion is never a good reason not to do the right thing, and we know that no matter how angry we are with someone,

we can still love and care for her. Being able to both express your immediate feelings and your overriding connection to your children reminds them that you love them no matter what and it offers insight into how their behavior affects others. I have been known to say, "I am so hurt by your choices right now, and I want you to know I love you and I hope you're able to make this right."

> Forgiveness means giving up all hope for a better past.—Lily Tomlin

I love this quote because it reminds me that what's done is done, and my job is to move forward and make the days to come even better. My relationship with my children will last for years to come, and if I can't forgive them for the mistakes they make as children, that will stand in the way of a strong, loving bond.

ACTIVITY: Kindness Questions

Taking some time to understand our instinctive reactions to certain situations can help us change the way we respond in the heat of the moment. Ask yourself the following questions:

- When is it hard for me to have compassion for others? When do I forget to bring kindness to a situation?
- When is it easy for me to be kind to others?
- What does this say about my assumptions and biases toward others?
- Has it always been like this for me, or was there a time when it was different?

Chapter Five

Shared Goals

It may seem obvious when our children are young that we all share similar goals. We want them to be healthy, happy, and find purpose in their lives, and mostly our children go along with the fundamental values we share without pushing back. But as they get older and start to make more choices, it can feel as though we aren't really all on the same page.

During the adolescent years, their job is to become individuals, find their passions, and develop their talents, but this can cause tension at home if you don't necessarily agree with how they spend their time and energy. Although it's not possible to come to consensus about everything, talking to our children about their goals and values is a good way to understand them better and try to find common ground. It's also a great way to validate their right to have their own ideas and practice advocating for themselves.

As teachers, we can slip into a mind-set that our goals are the only ones worth having, but that doesn't take into account all of the other things going on in teens and tweens lives. Not every child is determined to be on the honor roll. It's important to have the conversation with each student about his motivations and passions and what he hope to get out of our interactions before making assumptions.

It's also important to understand that often, youth this age are still working to identify what they want. Separating their family's wishes from what they think they "ought" to want and what it takes to fit in with their friends is a process, and it takes practice to develop the skill of self-inquiry, much less be honest with teachers and parents. The important part is the opportunity to practice asking themselves what they want and learning to own it without judgment.

> ACTIVITY: Four Questions
>
> Before there is conflict, it can be helpful to think about the answers to the following questions. Rather than acting on autopilot, or simply reacting to our children, having an idea of how you define your role in your teen's life can help you make more deliberate, purposeful decisions.
>
> 1. What is your parenting style? *This is not a question that should prompt judgment. Rather, it is designed to shine a light on the ways in which you interact with your children. Do you tend to leave them to their own devices most of the time and pick specific things or occasions to really home in on? For a variety of reasons, many parents let their children be fairly autonomous until there is a problem (grades slipping or someone gets caught shoplifting), and then they begin to pay closer attention or come down hard with punishment. Maybe you are the kind of parent who values peace above all and prefers to have a more friendly relationship with your child. Some parents tend to act out of fear, with lots of rules and restrictions and tight supervision. Others demand respect (children should be seen and not heard, my way or the highway), and still others are consistently middle-of-the-road when it comes to authority.*
> 2. What is your child's style? *Is your child strong willed and often defiant or questioning, or fairly compliant? Does he react strongly when things go wrong, or is the fairly relaxed? Does he rely on you for advice and life skills, or is he more independent? Is he withdrawn at home, or social and always in the thick of things? Once you've figured this out, set it up against your parenting style. No judgment—just observation. If you are a parent who wants to be your child's friend, but he is withdrawn at home, that might give you both some important information about the kinds of things that cause hurt feelings or conflict.*

3. What is your overall parenting goal? *When you think about what you want your parenting life to have been about, is it a peaceful home? A happy child? A financially successful child? One who is quiet and respectful of others? Do you hope for a close relationship with your adult child, or is it more important to you that shy leave home and forge her own path independently and not rely on you for help? What do you see being your main "job" as a parent? No answer is right or wrong.*
4. What are the barriers to those parenting goals? *Knowing what you now know about your parenting style and your child's style, are there things that you can imagine stand in the way of your main goals as a parent? This isn't about "fixing" anything yet; it's an exercise to help you get clarity with regard to relationship dynamics that might be dysfunctional.*

GROWTH VERSUS FIXED MIND-SET

Carol Dweck, a professor of psychology at Stanford University, has written a great deal about something she calls "mind-set" and how it affects our ability to be resilient and deal with challenges. Her work is based on the notion of two different mind-sets—fixed and growth. The fixed mind-set says that people are born with a particular level of intelligence that they will have forever. When we hear things such as, "He's good at math, but I'm not," or "No matter how much I study, I'm still going to fail this test," those are examples of a fixed mind-set.

Growth mind-set embraces the idea that hard work and effort are just as important as intelligence. People who believe in their ability to get better at things with practice and challenge themselves often have a growth mind-set. They are more likely to ask for help and find other ways to absorb knowledge and learn new things, and they tend to be happier and more able to bounce back from disappointments because, in general, they see obstacles as opportunities for growth.

Interestingly, many of us tend to have a growth mind-set when it comes to our children but not necessarily ourselves. We encourage our children to work hard—to practice piano or free throws or times tables, but many of us think we've reached our peak capacity for learning new things and either avoid things we've convinced ourselves we "are bad at," or give up when faced with harsh criticism.

Modeling a growth mind-set for our children can help them understand that, no matter our age or stage of life, we always have an opportunity to learn something new. When our children embrace the notion that they can do hard things with effort and creativity, they will feel more empowered and less overwhelmed by mistakes or failures.

Many schools have embraced this notion of growth mind-set, but it's important for teachers to also take into account context. Although it is important to emphasize to students that we all have the ability to grow and learn, it is also key to understand the circumstances of a child's life. Do family members at home support this idea? Do we understand enough about their learning and communication styles to help set them up for success? If we simply tell them that it's their job to believe in themselves and keep trying without helping them find effective ways to learn and grow, we have simply tossed a handful of seeds in their direction without watering or feeding them.

So, the most crucial ingredient here is the relationship between young people and the adults in their life. Yes, they need parents and teachers who believe in their ability to change and grow, and they need those adults to be there consistently, helping them understand their mistakes and glean the lessons from them.

Over a period of days, notice the kinds of things you praise your child or student for. Do you generally reward hard work and effort, or just outcomes, such as grades? Do you celebrate only when their team wins a game, or when you see them improve after every practice?

ACTIVITY: Growth versus Fixed Mind-Set Parenting

1. Listen to the kinds of things that go through your head when your child is struggling with something. Does the voice say, *"Science is just not this kid's thing,"* or does it say, *"Wow, she is working really hard but still struggling. I wonder if there's a different approach that we can find to help her understand this material?"*
2. How can you point this child toward opportunities for growth? Does he need a tutor or a mentor? Is there an older sibling or cousin who can walk him through a challenge

he's facing? Can you talk about growth as the natural outcome of failures rather than punishing your child for a mistake?
3. Pay attention to what you think when the child does triumph. Does the voice in your head say, *"You're such a natural at that!,"* or *"You worked so hard at this, and it's obviously paying off."*
4. Listen to the way your child talks about victories and challenges. Are there things he's given up on because he's convinced that he will never be good at them? Does he value his own hard work as much as the outcome he got?

Reframing for our children is incredibly important in a society where outcomes are valued as highly as they are. SAT scores and high-school transcripts, awards and accolades are held up as a sign that a child is on the right track, so if parents can counteract some of that at home and remind children that other considerations are just as important (although much less visible), we can help them feel a little more balanced.

Another caveat to the idea of a growth mind-set is this: many of the systems our children navigate every day have built-in biases, so children who are not neurotypical or have a physical disability or don't otherwise fit the characteristics of the dominant culture will experience the definition of "success" in a very different way. The goal is *not* to force them to assimilate to the dominant culture.

Validating children's experience is paramount, and helping them come to some realization that their effort and work are important regardless of how others define them will serve them well. Letting teens and tweens come up with their own idea of what success looks like and acknowledging their unique talents and gifts is key.

MISTAKES

How we react when children make mistakes is really important, because it teaches them how to react to themselves when they mess up. It's good to remember that nobody is born knowing how to do everything; and often, we have to try things several times before we really understand what's going wrong or where we can do better.

The goal of learning is not to reach a point where we have amassed enough knowledge that we will never make a mistake again. Learning is a lifelong process, but if our approach to mistakes is to feel shame and embarrassment, we are less likely to learn from them.

The image below can help us think about the different kind of mistakes we make and how likely we are to learn from them:

Sloppy mistakes happen when we aren't really paying attention. Thus, the intentionality is low, and the learning potential isn't as high, either. But that doesn't mean we don't learn from these things. Often, we make those kinds of mistakes, and they force us to start focusing, which is generally good. Unfortunately, often, these mistakes are accompanied by embarrassment or being mocked.

High-stakes scenarios where we make mistakes often mean that we are very intentional about what we are doing, but also, because our emotions are so tied to the outcome, when we falter, we tend to focus less on the potential for learning from that incident and more on how upset we are over what we lost as a result.

Aha moments are times when we are either messing around, or we stumble on a solution without really trying to. Because these are often happy mistakes, our frame of mind means that we learn a lot from these

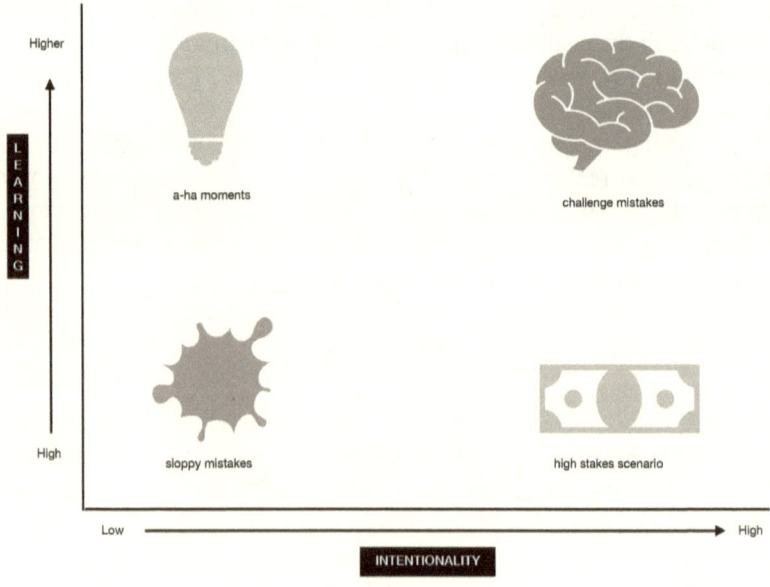

Figure 5.1. Learning versus intentionality graph. *Kari L. O'Driscoll*

incidents. Positivity and curiosity lead to learning because we are often pleasantly surprised with aha moments.

Challenge mistakes happen when we work really hard to figure out something and use the information about what's not working to inform ideas of what might work. Helping children frame the kinds of mistakes they're making can help them decide how to learn from them. The more we respond positively and with support, the more likely children are to gain knowledge and be willing to keep trying. Sometimes, all it takes is for us to shift our perspective to get them back on the right track.

Mistakes are emotional. Nobody wants to fail, and if failing leads us gradually to become unwilling to try again, we're giving up opportunities to learn. Below are some ideas of things we can encourage children to try when they're frustrated with a task or challenge:

INSTEAD OF:	TRY:
Assigning blame	Letting it go and moving forward
Spending too much time describing the problem	Assessing the first issue and identifying who you can ask for help
Feeling stuck	Moving your body and thinking outside the box
Trying to force it by doing the same thing over again	Slightly tweaking the process and trying again, or blowing it up altogether and starting fresh
Half-assing it just to be done	Finding a partner to work with or taking a break and coming back to it
Abandoning it or giving up	Acknowledging your frustration, deciding whether this has to be done right now (or at all), and maybe letting all or part of it go

VALUES

Part of sharing goals with another person is understanding what is truly important to them and helping them understand what's important to you. It may feel as though your values are obvious to your child or students, but unless we ask, we won't know if our behavior and choices are saying what we think they are.

Children might see us overwhelmed by work during most of our waking hours and believe that our job is more important than our family. You may spend a lot of time and energy making sure the house is in order and the yard is presentable because you want your family to have a calm, peaceful place to live, but children may interpret that as us caring more about cleanliness than connecting with them.

When we are motivated by internal values and guidance, we are happier and more creative. When the majority of the things we do are in service to external goals (more money, keeping up with coworkers, proving ourselves to others), we may be productive and "successful," but we are also disconnected from ourselves, and we risk losing sight of the things that make us happy and excited.

All of us need to have a sense of what we love doing, where we want to spend our energy and time, because many of our external motivations are rooted in lack and fear. If you work hard because you are afraid of not having enough money, losing your job, or not being able to maintain your status, your body is on constant alert. The physiological response to fear is designed to be short-lived, not chronic.

When we understand which choices make us feel fulfilled, what interests us, and what pulls us to get out of bed in the morning, we act from passion and desire and a sense of hope. Even if your financial circumstances don't enable you to do work you love, it is possible to find time and energy to do things you find fun, or at least begin to plan how to balance your time more evenly.

It can be hard to prioritize thinking about values and passions and dreams because we are so consumed with the duties of parenting and paid work. You can start to spur your curiosity by answering the following questions. Take your time and have fun with it; the clearer you are on what drives you and makes you unique, the more you'll be able to relate to your child or student on that same level.

If your teens or tweens are willing to answer the questions and share their responses with you, this can be a powerful way to connect. Gaining insight into their view of themselves and offering them the same view of you can create deeper understanding of each other's motivations and behaviors. The added bonus is that it may prompt you to discover mutual interests you can pursue together, or at least learn about from each other.

ACTIVITY: Values Worksheet

- What are your favorite things to do?
- Who are your favorite people? Why?
- If you had to choose between two events happening on the same night, how would you decide?
- What is your default emotion?
- What sorts of things make you terribly angry?
- What sorts of things make you terribly sad?
- What sorts of things make you immeasurably happy?
- What could you do without for the rest of your life?
- What are you most afraid of losing?

This next activity can also illustrate some of what we value about each other in our households. You may need to demonstrate it yourself for a while before others begin to engage with it, but it never feels bad to have someone acknowledge you and call out your good qualities. When everyone is in a hurry, stressed about homework and quizzes, their position on the team and getting food on the table, it can be hard to remember what we like about each other. Rather, we tend to focus on how the people we live with get in our way or make things harder for us.

ACTIVITY: Appreciation Board

You can post a large sheet of paper or chalkboard/whiteboard somewhere in a common area of the house—the kitchen or family room. Write everyone's name at the top of the board with the beginning of a sentence beneath it like this:

I generally kick things off by quietly circling one person's name and finishing the sentence before anyone else gets up for the day. For example, I might circle Markus's name and write "is so awesome because he is such a good friend to his friends."

It always feels good to be called out in a good way, and over time, the children take the initiative and call out each other for positive things. The guidelines I have for the Appreciation Board in our house are:

- It can be anonymous if you want.
- Each message stays up for a minimum of three days.

- Only positive, supportive messages are left up.
- Messages that reflect someone's personal qualities are preferred (as opposed to specific acts), but those are welcome, too, especially if they speak to their best qualities.

I love this simple way of reminding my children that looking for others' positive attributes is powerful. So often, our communication at home centers around things we need done or conflicts we have, so shining a light on the things we take for granted about each other is a great way to build family unity.

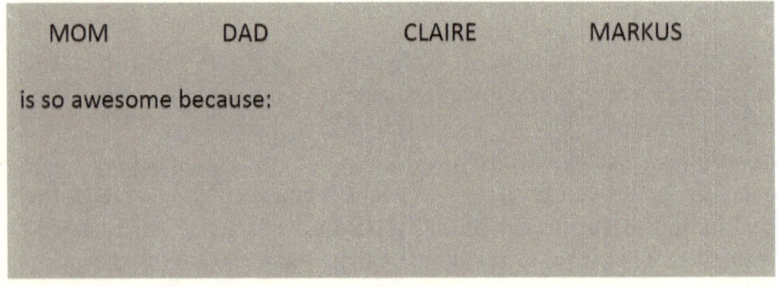

Figure 5.2.   Family self-esteem booster. *Kari L. O'Driscoll*

Chapter Six

Conflict

> Healthy families resolve conflict without coercion, shaming or violence. They cooperate, help their kids individuate, and strive to meet all collective and individual needs. —bell hooks

If you have or work with children, you have conflict. No relationship is perfect in terms of everyone agreeing on how or when to do things, but given the changing nature of relationships as children grow up, and the emotional volatility of the adolescent years, relationships can get particularly complicated.

Although we can't eliminate conflict, we can learn to get better at addressing it and maintaining our relationships and our integrity. Some of us were raised to avoid conflict at all costs, but that makes it difficult to connect with others in a way that is genuine. Even when it's uncomfortable, it's important to learn how to have respectful conversations with people when we disagree, and giving children practice at disagreeing in positive ways increases critical thinking skills and emotional maturity.

Generally, conflict is about power—who has it and who wants it. When we don't particularly care about the outcome, we won't really fight for it, but when we want something or believe we deserve something, we will often fight to the end. The trick as a parent or teacher is to determine who wants what and why, rather than simply asserting our power as the adult in charge.

When power struggles start, it is normal and natural to set aside the real issue in favor of "winning." It's possible to lay down the law and be rigid about it, but as children get older, they develop clever ways to get what they want. In general, if I forbid my adolescents to have or do something without any conversation about it, they are more likely to sneak around and try to get it without me knowing than they are to bow to my authority. Remember, their job during these years is to assert their independence, and our job is to give them boundaries and healthy ways to do that.

Constructive conflict lies in the ability and the willingness to see others' perspectives. Parents can model perspective taking for children, but that is really hard to do when emotions are high, which is why mindfulness is important. We need to feel ourselves getting upset, take a moment to let the primary wave of emotion subside, get curious about why we feel that way, and try to understand where the other person is coming from. Only then do we have the presence of mind to ask what our children are asking for and why.

THE DIFFERENCE BETWEEN CONFLICT AND DISAGREEMENT

As noted above, conflict is about power. Think about a time when you disagreed with someone, and you didn't cross the threshold of being a little annoyed to being angry. I like to give the example of pizza toppings to help illustrate this concept. We might agree that we both really love pizza, but your favorite is Canadian bacon and pineapple, whereas I prefer pepperoni and goat cheese. It's pretty unlikely that we will have a conflict over it, though, because even if we can only order one pizza, we can get one-half with your preferred toppings and the other half with mine. In this scenario, we both have power and agency.

Conflict arises when we disagree about something and one person has the power to decide for everyone. If I'm the person without power, I will fight fiercely to convince you that I'm right, to get power to decide for myself. The issue becomes emotional because when I don't have the ability to make my own choices, I feel trapped.

As children hit the teen years, it is harder and harder for us to control their choices, even if we think we have power over them. We can tell them their curfew is 11 p.m. and let them know there will be consequences if they break that rule, but unless we are willing or able physically to keep them from leaving the house after that time or find them and bring them home, they have power they didn't have previously. That causes conflict, because both of us want power. So how do we share power with our children as they get older?

GOING BEYOND "NO"

When my oldest daughter was in fourth grade, the Twilight books were very popular. Erin went to school with several girls who had older sisters, and many of them were reading these books. At the time, in our house, we were knee-deep in the Harry Potter series, and I was really excited that Erin was so enthusiastic about reading.

One day, she came home from school and asked if she could read the first Twilight book. I was a little nervous because I thought that it was a bit too mature for her, but she worked hard to make her case. She told me about all of her friends who were reading them, talked about one friend whose older sister had them all and offered to loan them to her, and she said that the elementary school library even had them.

I had a choice to make. I knew that if I said no, my strong-willed daughter would likely find a way to get them without telling me. The school librarian's policy was to let any student check out any book as a way to encourage reading for pleasure. I also knew that Erin would continue to work me until I said yes—she didn't give up easily on anything.

I asked her to wait a few days while I thought about it and, ultimately, I made her a deal. We would read the first book together—book club style. This would give me the opportunity to talk with her about the content every couple of chapters so that we could address some of the more mature themes in the book. Although I wasn't interested in the book for my own purposes, it was a way to see what she was getting out of it and injecting my parental values into the mix. She agreed.

We lasted about five chapters. The more we read together, the more she realized that this wasn't her kind of book. Many of the romantic themes flew over her head at the age of ten (thank goodness), and the rest was so poorly written when compared to Harry Potter that she became frustrated. The more we talked, the more she opened up about her real reason for wanting to read it, which was to be able to talk to her friends about it at lunch and "fit in."

Ultimately, she decided it wasn't worth it to slog through a book that she didn't enjoy, and she abandoned it in favor of other activities she could do with her friends. Putting aside my desire to wield authority over her by saying no gave me the opportunity to connect with her in a way that gave her freedom but helped her examine her values and motivation. Had I simply said no, I'm certain she would have read it anyway; and even if she had still given up on it, conflict certainly would have arisen when I found out that she'd defied me.

Different types of conflict arise, to be sure. The easiest ones to handle are the ones that give me time to think—the request to go to a party over the weekend, or go to an R-rated movie. I've taught my children that I need time to make those kinds of decisions, and they can't expect me to answer right away. Buying time to decide lets me acknowledge my initial gut reaction and question why I feel so strongly one way or another.

Conflict is rooted in emotion, and when the emotion centers of our brain are in full force, we are in fight/flight/fear response. Especially during the adolescent years, this response is overwhelming, so entering into conflict with our children without settling our own emotional response is setting us up for trouble. When emotions are high, the portion of the brain that learns shuts down, and in order to resolve disagreements with people we love in a way that feels healthy and productive, we have to be willing and able to learn from each other.

Not only do we need to allow time for our emotions to settle, but we have to wait for our children to do the same. When one person is calm and the other is emotionally fired up, no connecting through dialogue is possible. That is not to say that an emotional response is wrong or inappropriate, just that conflict resolution can't happen until the emotions are acknowledged and less intense. Personally, I have never said anything out of extreme anger that I later felt good about saying, especially to someone I am in relationship with.

> ACTIVITY: Defusing Your Anger
>
> When volatile situations arise, try to go through the following steps yourself and with your child so that you can process the strong feelings and move to a place where conversation and learning are constructive.
>
> - Recognize the signs of extreme emotion such as anger *(chest tight, heart racing, face flushed, hands and jaw clenched).*

- Acknowledge that you have a choice between **reacting** *(doesn't involve thought)* and **responding** *(thoughtful, calm, reasoned)*.
- Breathe deeply into your belly and out through your mouth for several rounds.
- Ask yourself why you think you're so upset. Examine your assumptions. Where is your brain "filling in the gaps"?
- Stay curious about what you're afraid of in this situation, and acknowledge that most of our worst fears never come to pass.
- Identify your goal in this situation. Can there be common ground?
- Express your feelings and own them *(I'm really angry right now* instead of *you're pissing me off)*.

TAKING IT PERSONALLY

I can't imagine ever forgetting the first time my daughter said the words "I *hate* you" to me. She was three years old, and it was gut wrenching. She's twenty-one now, and although I can look back on it and understand that she was working out ways to claim power and get what she wanted, that she wasn't articulate enough to express her strong feelings, it really hurt. It took me years to figure out how not to take her verbal attacks personally.

The older she got, the better she was at pushing my buttons and saying things she knew would hit at the core of who I am. But if I follow my own teaching, I have to remember that the things other people do and say are about them, not about me. I have to remind myself that just because someone is angry with me or doesn't like me, that doesn't mean I'm a horrible person. Just because everyone doesn't love me all the time doesn't mean I'm unlovable.

It is also important to remember that children are emotional beings, and they are experimenting and working out the power of words. They also experience strong emotions that will subside if we don't engage and amp them up, and it's our job to acknowledge our children's right to feel what they feel, maintain boundaries around how they treat us, and let them know that we care for them, no matter what.

To be certain, I draw the line at hateful words and acts of physical violence and destruction. When one of my children yells at me, I wait until she is done, let her know that I deserve to be treated with respect and kindness, and that I am open to talking later when the strongest emotions have passed and she is ready to listen to me as well as talk about what's going on.

One of my daughters is generally determined to engage in the moment. It can be a struggle to walk away and get some space, but I don't have to engage just because she wants to; ultimately, I hope that I'm setting the example for her that she has the right to request space for herself, too. My other daughter hates conflict and tends to explode in anger and be done quickly. Often, when I check in later, she apologizes and says she's moved on.

When we take our children's words personally, we can inflate the conflict because we tend to get defensive and hurt. Often, this results in us exerting power over them in retaliation or becoming invested in "winning" instead of getting to the core of the issue. The argument has suddenly become about you versus me, and it is hard to find common ground.

If you can cultivate the ability to not take their words personally, it will be harder for them to make the fight about right/wrong or pitting hurt feelings against each other. It is hard, and it takes a lot of practice, especially if you are close to your children, and they know you well enough to know what will hurt you most.

At times I completely forget all of this and just stew in my pain, but if I'm paying attention and staying curious about my strong emotions, I've learned to identify that if I feel

- defensive,
- self-righteous, or
- blaming,

I am taking it personally. If I feel the need to justify my choices or amazed at how I am taken for granted or if I start a sentence with name calling or put-downs, it's time to step back and get some space because I'm making it about me. That will get us nowhere.

ACTIVITY: Three Questions

When I am overwhelmed with emotion and tempted to lash out at my teen, I try to stop and ask myself three questions before I start yelling or handing out punishments. The questions come from Dr. Brené Brown's book *Daring Greatly*. The answers are mine.

1. Do I have enough information about this situation to make a decision? *Almost every time, the answer is no, especially if I have walked into the middle of my daughters fighting with each other, or if I've only heard the teacher's account of events. Chances are, I need way more information. My child isn't always the most reliable source of information, but the best thing I can do before blowing up is ask lots of questions.*
2. Am I fully present? *If the situation has taken me by surprise, the answer to this question is, generally, no. If I'm in the middle of making dinner or paying bills or rushing out the door, and my daughters erupt in a screaming match, my brain is somewhere else, and I'm more likely to be irritated and impatient because I want to be doing something else. If I can't be fully present by stopping what I am doing and paying 100 percent attention with a clear head and a calm demeanor, I'm will only make things worse. Nobody benefits from me being distracted or rushing things.*
3. What am I afraid of? *This one is huge, because it generally dictates how I respond. It takes a lot of practice, but the more I ask myself this question and really dig deep to understand the answer, the more I understand how my fears can drive my parenting. Some of the most common things I fear as a parent are:*

- *Raising snotty, entitled children other people will dislike,*
- *That someone will get physically injured,*
- *That this means I'm not a good parent, or it's somehow my "fault," and*
- *That my child will go somewhere and do something really stupid and ruin the rest of her life.*

More often than not, the things we fear the most are the ones least likely to happen. Human beings tend to predict things in best- or worst-case scenarios even though the vast majority of outcomes happen somewhere in the middle. By taking a moment to assess my fears, I can get a reality check. We hear so many catastrophic stories about teens and substance use, depression, pregnancy, and more, and we tend to focus on those stories when we're in conflict with our children.

We are driven to protect them, and the more independent they get, the more out of control we feel. And the more out of control we feel, the more likely we are to close ranks and keep everyone as close as we can, but our children, who are driven to explore, take risks, and become more independent, feel claustrophobic when we do this. And the message we're sending is that we don't trust them to make good choices, but it's our job to help them develop that skill, not keep them from doing it at all until they move out.

As teachers, we can feel as though it is our job to be in control at all times, and we can be driven by fears of a classroom out of control, or students harming themselves or others. It may often feel easier to "outsource" the problem by sending a child out of the classroom, but it's important to be able to discern when that is a necessary consequence and when we can instead connect with a student. The most impactful thing we can do as educators is build relationship with our students and establish trust.

SETTING BOUNDARIES

Parents and teachers are people, too, and we get our feelings hurt, we feel disrespected or disregarded, and we sometimes don't handle it very well. We have the right to set boundaries with everyone we are in relationship with so that they understand how we want to be treated. It is perfectly OK to acknowledge that someone is angry and hurting *and* refuse to let ourselves be harmed emotionally or physically.

There may be situations where setting boundaries feels incredibly difficult—a child who struggles with addiction, one who physically harms a sibling or classmate, or if they are not treating you in a way that is kind and respectful of your needs. This is all the more reason for you to make your boundaries known.

Caring deeply for someone else does not require us to become so depleted (emotionally, financially, physically, or otherwise) that we are unable to function and center our own well-being. It also does not demand that we show up for and take on every argument. It is, however, incumbent upon us to be very clear about what our boundaries are so that the other person knows.

I developed the following set of rules for hard conversations when my daughters were teens because they are very different people with different emotional triggers and communication styles. Knowing that anger keeps us from communicating with intention and effectively, I wanted us to be able to talk about emotionally difficult things without devolving into chaos.

Rules for Hard Conversations

1. Everyone at the table is here because they want to be, not because they are forced to be or shamed/guilted into it. *Force and shame/guilt set up a power dynamic that dooms the discussion to failure before it starts.*
2. Everyone has the same rights; we are all equals, and we all deserve to be heard and have our perspectives honored. *It doesn't matter how old someone is or their status in the family. We have no trump cards if we are truly interested in working through and finding a solution that works for everyone. If someone thinks that he is bound to be overruled at some point, he won't even try. If anyone believes he alone has the power to decide the ultimate outcome, he won't listen to anyone else.*
3. Even if we can't understand someone else's point of view or feelings, we respect their right to have them, and we all agree not to mock or belittle them for seeing things that way. *No gaslighting. Your reaction might seem disproportionate or even absurd to me, but because I'm not living in your skin, I don't get to tell you how to feel, and I certainly don't get to shame you for feeling that way.*
4. No name calling, ultimatums, demands, or hate speech. *This might seem obvious, but when we get into situations that seem to be going nowhere, we often resort to these kinds of tactics in order to ratchet up the urgency and make others meet our emotional state. But it is important to remember that if we truly want to solve a problem, we can't use this to trigger emotion and shut down conversation.*
5. We all agree to work our hardest to define a common goal and work toward it. Bringing up past resentments is not OK. *Patterns of past behavior may exist and feel relevant, but if we are to have a conversation about the issue that presents itself right now, we all need to stay in this moment. Blaming or shaming*

someone for previous acts is not helpful to this particular issue in any way.
6. No eye rolling, turning away, or other negative or dismissive body language. *This kind of behavior sends the message that you are not listening or truly interested in understanding where the other person is coming from. If either of those things is true, you have no reason to be part of the conversation.*
7. If someone decides he cannot be part of the conversation right now for any reason, he is allowed to leave but agree to come back to it in the near future so that it won't remain unresolved. *Sometimes, people get so emotionally triggered that they know staying with it won't be productive, but it doesn't excuse them from being part of the solution at some point. It is perfectly acceptable to ask for and receive accommodation in the future to avoid triggers (writing, having an advocate sit with you, taking breaks to walk around the block, etc.).*
8. Everyone agrees to own his part of the issue and take responsibility for his words and actions that might have resulted in pain or frustration for others. *Every conflict has multiple sides. Nobody is ever all right or all wrong.*
9. Avoid blaming and shaming, labeling someone, and using words such as "always" and "never," which will not move us forward. *These are all shortcuts to ending difficult conversations and an indication that you are making assumptions about the other person's character or intent. That will get us nowhere.*

DISCIPLINE VERSUS PUNISHMENT

It is common for parents of teens to be hyper-focused on discipline, partially because the stakes are so much higher when children hit middle and high school. It is not just about staying in bed and sharing your toys anymore; we can be plagued with worries about school suspensions, shoplifting, underage drinking.

One important thing to remember is that discipline is about learning. It isn't about revenge or punishment or even safety (although we definitely want our children to be safe). Adolescence is a time when it is vital that we help our children learn to make better choices. To do that, we have to focus on teaching them as much as possible even (and especially) when they aren't receptive to it.

Punishment is more about retribution or protecting our children in the short term, but if we really want them to develop the ability to learn from their mistakes, we have to dedicate ourselves to discipline instead of punishment. The tricky thing with children this age is figuring out how to do that within the context of their brain development.

It is key that we remember the basics of adolescent brain and emotional development. During times of stress and conflict, remembering that the tween/teen brain isn't quite yet up to the task of performing like an adult brain will help everyone. We tend to view power and control as a way to feel safe and secure, but it is much more complicated than that and, knowing that children will increasingly bristle under our control, it is important to develop ways to work with them when things go sideways.

This figure shows one way to address issues and work through disagreements. Maybe you want your children to have an early curfew, but they want it to be later. What happens if you play with different ways of doing it—maybe they want to see how things go if they call and tell you where they are when they're out and, for that specific scenario, you decide together what time is acceptable. Maybe they have a different curfew for summer evenings than they do during the school year. Using this method, as your child grows up and gains more independence, the two of you can work together to be flexible and responsive to both your needs.

This works in the classroom, too, if the system just doesn't seem to work for some students. Involving students in the process of brainstorming and experimenting about how to tweak it so that it is easier to manage shows that you care about their experience and that you're willing to help them develop problem-solving skills.

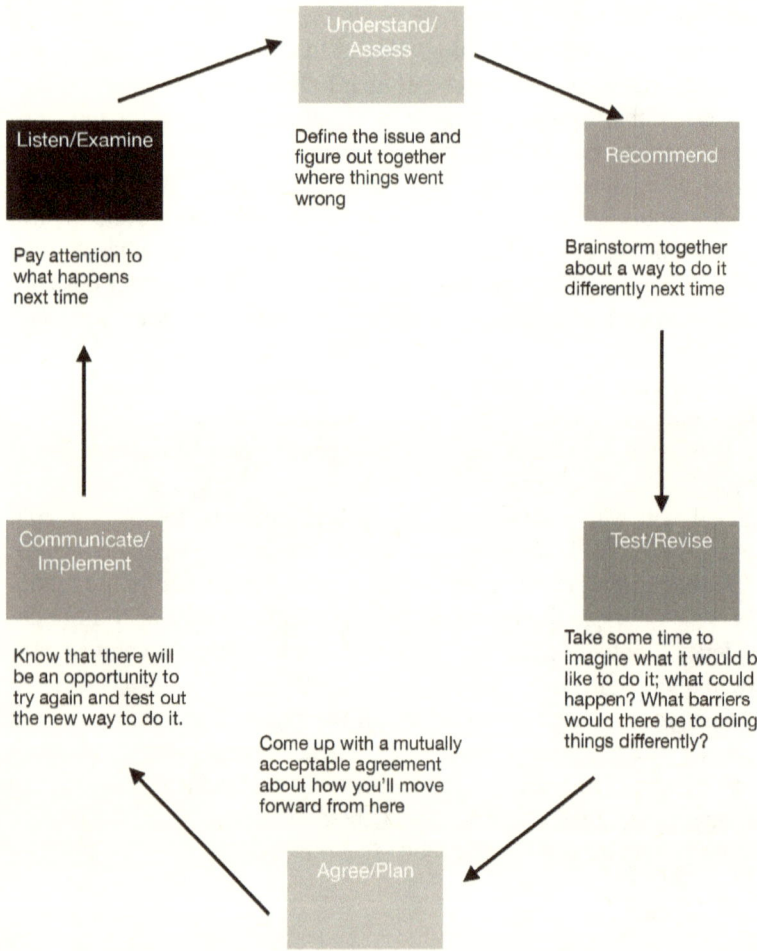

Figure 6.1. Collaborative Problem Solving. *Kari L. O'Driscoll*

Chapter Seven

Adolescent Health and Well-Being

By many accounts, today's teens are more stressed out than any other generation in modern history. They are more plagued with depression and anxiety disorders, their rates of suicide and self-harm behaviors are unprecedented, and it's frankly not hard to understand why. Never before have there been so many standardized tests, the competition to get into college is heated and intense, rates of poverty have skyrocketed, and in many schools, children are being sent home with hours and hours of homework every night. Add the stress of adolescent emotions and hormones to this, and you have a perfect storm.

According to Dr. Rick Hanson, well-being consists of four components:

1. awareness
2. connection
3. insight
4. purpose

When we are aware of our surroundings and our own bodies, feel connected to others around us, have insight into our motivations and values and learning process, and are clear on our purpose, we feel calm and grounded. Just as mindfulness practices help us as parents, they help our children move through the world with intention and optimism. Mindfulness can also help our children develop self-compassion during a time when so many of them feel bad about themselves.

When our children see themselves with kindness versus judgment, experience their entire humanity and understand that they belong to others versus feeling isolated and alone, they are more likely to manage challenges with optimism and see themselves in a positive way.

So how do we help our children? What can we do to guide them through these challenging times with some semblance of calm and optimism?

UNDERSTAND AND EXPLAIN THE BRAIN'S DEAD ENDS

Some thoughts and patterns of thought lead us to virtual dead-ends in our heads. They literally box us in and shut down critical thinking and optimism, and the more we indulge in those thoughts, the harder it is to change them. Wearing pathways in our brain that lead to sadness, isolation, and anxiety makes it easier and easier to travel those routes. What you practice grows stronger, even with regard to neural development.

When we find ourselves thinking this way, we tend to push other people away, dwell on negative possibilities, and react to others instead of responding to them. When we don't engage with others socially, we don't benefit from other perspectives and have a hard time seeing opportunities or possibilities, much less hear ideas that counteract our unhappy thoughts. These can show up as

- self-doubt
- fear
- scarcity *(I'm not good enough, there isn't enough time, I'll never have enough . . .)*
- impatience with ourselves
- hopelessness
- lack of purpose

The good news is, we can get ourselves out of those dark, lonely places, and the more we can practice substituting these thoughts for others, the easier it gets. Every time you notice your child heading into that dark place, think about whether you can help her with one or more of the following:

- Mindfulness without judgment *(Recognize what is happening—are you doubting yourself or feeling afraid? Often the simple act of*

naming what you're feeling has the effect of decreasing the intensity of the feeling.)
- Self-compassion *(Human beings make mistakes and get afraid. It's how we learn, and it's not just OK: it's literally required. Nobody was born knowing how to do everything.)*
- Cultivate purpose and meaning *(What is most important to me in my life? What are my goals? What do I value? How can I focus on that right now? Even if I'm terrified, can I turn it around to think about valuing courage and continuing to move forward in the face of doubt?)*
- Play *(Take time to do something for the sheer joy of it. Play unleashes creativity and helps us pay attention to something whose only goal is to have fun.)*
- Understand complexity *(Remember that completing patterns and figuring out something gives us a hit of dopamine. Do a puzzle or teaching someone else how to do something you're really good at as a way to remind yourself how capable you are.)*

Things that offer possibility, open up ideas, and connect us with other people have a way of getting us out of thought patterns that defeat us. The more we experience the world of options opening up to us, the happier we will be.

NOTICING HOW YOUR STRESS AND YOUR CHILD'S STRESS FEED EACH OTHER

Emotions are contagious, so even if we don't notice it happening, we can fall into the trap of amplifying someone else's feelings. That's great when we're experiencing joy, but it can lead to disaster when we fuel someone else's frustration or anxiety.

One night, after a particularly challenging day of racing from work to school to after-school activities, jetting home to make dinner and clean up and generally feeling overwhelmed at the thought of one more day of single parenting, I wanted nothing more than to collapse on the couch with the TV remote for some "me time."

My youngest, then about eleven years old, called me to sit with her for a few minutes as she fell asleep. She was having a hard time calming down and was teary and whiny, and I got snarky. I told her she had the tools to figure it out, I was tired, and I headed out to tell her sister goodnight.

My oldest, who had been sick with a nasty cold for a couple of weeks, stuck her tongue out for me to examine as soon as I walked into her room. She wanted to know whether she should worry about the white rash in her mouth. I sighed loudly and told her it was nothing to worry about and rolled my eyes when she told me she'd gone searching on the internet and learned about all the horrible, mysterious diseases it could mean she had. She was panicked and wanted me to take her to the doctor immediately.

My youngest was audibly still upset in her room, and I threw up my hands and walked out of the room, ignoring both girls. I convinced myself I was letting them "tough it out," and they would be fine. We all went to bed unhappy.

In both cases, the real issue was my inability to identify my own stress and set it aside before I interacted with my children. My exhaustion and fears about sustaining my own energy levels weighed so heavily on my mind that I couldn't separate them out and piled their fears and anxiety on top of mine. Then I made the choice to throw it all out in one instant.

Instead of sitting with each girl for a few minutes, acknowledging their emotional needs and brainstorming ways to help them feel more in control and relaxed, I succumbed to my own discomfort and shut down, which didn't help anyone. I was feeling their angst as I sat in their rooms, and they were feeling mine, but instead of acknowledging it and empathizing with each other, we just made it worse for all of us.

Of course, both of my girls fell asleep that night, as did I, but I didn't reinforce the message that they could rely on me or confide in me when they were scared or anxious. I "told" them that their feelings didn't matter, that I couldn't handle them, and that the solution was to give up. That's not ultimately the kind of parent I strive to be, and I never want my children to feel like they can't come to me with something important because I will dismiss them.

As an adult, my job is to know that when my children ask for help, they are being courageous. When I refuse to help them because their stress makes me uncomfortable, I'm undermining the relationship and eroding trust. That doesn't mean I don't have a right to feel anxious or overwhelmed, just that it's important to not let that get in the way of connecting with someone who needs me.

ACTIVITY: Assess Your Stress

1. Try to recall a time when you were unable or unwilling to find empathy because of your stress level.
2. What triggers your stress response? What are your children's triggers?
3. What is your baseline stress level on an average day? What do you think your partner or children would say it is?
4. How do you generally respond to stress? How do your partner and children respond to your stress?
5. Can you try to set aside your stressors when your children need your help to destress? What can you do or say to yourself that might allow you to be available to them without the weight of your own pressures?

DEALING WITH AN UNEXPECTED EVENT

One way to avoid stress is to resist change. If we can just keep things predictable and avoid situations where we aren't in control, we feel more safe and secure. Unfortunately, that's not how life works, so it's up to us to learn how to adapt to change and handle unexpected events that challenge us. For our children, these can be things such as being disciplined by a coach or receiving a failing score on a school project. And often, our children won't want to talk to us about how this makes them feel, instead going into catastrophic thinking patterns or dead ends in their own heads. It's important to help them remember a few key things:

- Naming what you feel in the moment often decreases the intensity of the feeling.
- If we don't start to build stories around our emotions or fears, the strongest emotions will begin to dissipate on their own in about ninety seconds.
- Worst-case scenarios rarely happen.
- Nobody thinks about you or makes fun of you nearly as much as you imagine they do.

It's tempting to commiserate with our children to show support when they're upset, but sometimes that just validates a "poor-me" attitude.

Some parents also love going to bat for their children. Although it's absolutely appropriate to advocate for our children in certain situations, reacting to our children' disappointments by saying, "You're right, that isn't fair," or "Anna was a horrible partner for that project—you did all the work!" indicates that they are victims without any control over what happens to them. Unfortunately, although that might feel good in the moment, it sets them up for a passive existence and strips them of power in their own lives.

Offering to rush in and make things better sends the message that you don't think they're capable of taking care of difficult situations on their own. Helping children acknowledge their emotions, assess whether this is situation requires action, and helping them brainstorm ideas to mitigate disaster and learn self-advocacy is ultimately the way to learn whatever lessons they can from this unhappy event.

HELPING ADOLESCENTS FIND MEANING

Teens and tweens are inundated with goals nearly every day. Unfortunately, most of them come from external sources—coaches, teachers, parents, employers. If they are to be seen as "successful," they have to live up to many different standards that other people set, which can make it hard to identify what is important to them. When you're surrounded by people telling you what you "ought" to do, it's easy to go on autopilot to meet expectations and lose touch with your own motivations and values.

A lot of research shows that we feel better about the things we do when they're tied to some internal purpose. It has been called the IKEA effect—that we value things much more if we make them ourselves or have some hand in their creation. It gives us a sense of ownership and power to know that we did something because we wanted to, rather than because we were told to.

> ACTIVITY: Tackling Tough Situations
> Sometimes, when we find ourselves in a challenging time, we react with anger or frustration. Other times, we are tempted to shove our unpleasant emotions aside and just keep going, even though ignoring them rarely works for very long. The next time your child is struggling with a difficult situation, encourage him to sit down with you and look over this flowchart.

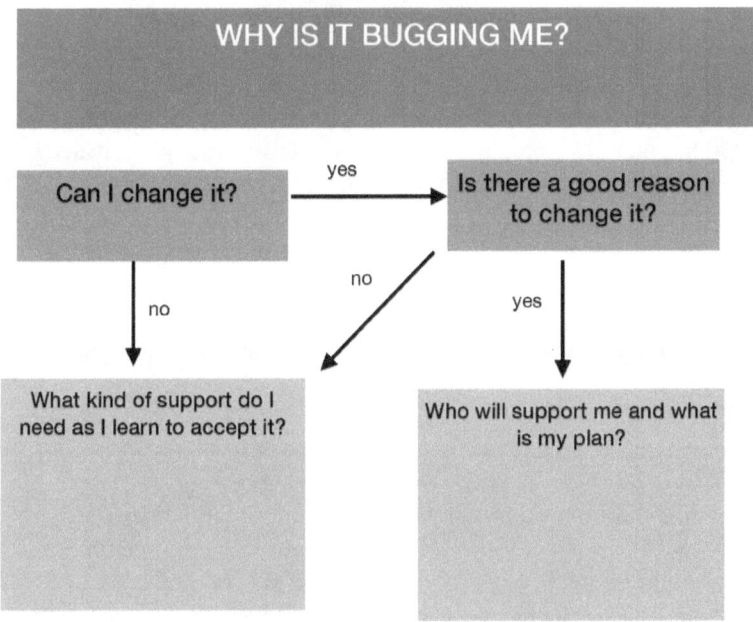

The first two boxes give them an opportunity to describe what is happening and become aware of the emotional reaction they're having to it. Making their way through the flow chart, they begin to see that it's possible to make choices about how to respond with intention. This is a powerful and quick reminder that we are always in charge of how we deal with the situations we find ourselves in. By the end of the worksheet, your child is prompted to made a conscious choice to either accept what has happened and move on, or reach out for help in an effort to make things better.

Figure 7.1. Identifying sources of stress flowchart. *Kari L. O'Driscoll*

When we help children this age begin to define their personal values and goals, framing conversations in terms of what is important to them and why, it can help them understand what matters to them and help focus their time and energy. It can also inject their daily lives with a little more energy and joy.

ACTIVITY: Do Your Activities Have Meaning?

This is great for teens or tweens to do on their own or as a conversation starter so that they can bounce ideas off of you, and you can hear their thoughts.

- How much of your day is spent doing things that you don't feel are important? How often do you do things to please other people without really being personally invested in the outcome?
- Do you think you are more internally or externally motivated? Does it depend on what you're doing? If there are times when it varies, do you notice a difference in your level of enthusiasm for a task when you're doing something creative or "meaningful"?
- When you are stressed or anxious, how often is it due to an outside expectation that you think you can't or don't want to meet?

ACTIVITY: Help Your Child Plan for Success

Sometimes, even though we know what is important to us, it is hard to know exactly how to begin. Some tasks feel enormous, and others incredibly complicated, even if we are motivated to do them. When I feel myself getting worried about an upcoming deadline, I find the following exercise really helpful in focusing my attention and being mindful of my reasons for doing it.

1. Set an achievable goal. *(I want to get an A on my next English paper. I want to get more assists in the next basketball game.)*
2. What will happen if I achieve this goal? *(My parents will stop nagging me and see that I'm working hard. I might make the varsity basketball team next year.)*
3. Why is this important to me? *(I want my parents to trust that I'm serious about my education. I really love basketball, and the varsity coach can help me develop my skills.)*
4. Be realistic about what it will take to meet this goal. Identify potential obstacles and plan for them. Build in flexibility in case something happens that you can't predict. *(I have to work after school this week, and we are going out*

> *of town this weekend, so I have to find other times to prepare for this paper. I might not play a lot in the next game, but maybe if I tell my coach my goal, he will put me in more.)*
> 5. Decide what realistic progress looks like. *(I got a C on my last paper, so I guess if I get a B this time, at least that's an improvement, and I know I can keep working. Even if I get the same number of assists or just one more in the next game, I'll know that I'm on the right track.)*

This is a great way for children to begin exerting control over important things in their lives. When we are clear about what we want and why we want it, we can move forward with conviction and purpose. Being honest about our abilities and the obstacles in our way helps us plan, be flexible, and feel empowered. When we make choices based on what is important to us, we are ultimately happier and more resilient.

HELP ADOLESCENTS FEEL LIKE THEY'RE PART OF SOMETHING BIGGER

Children this age can get lost in their own world, thinking mostly about themselves and worrying about how others see them. This is perfectly normal, developmentally speaking, but the longer we live inside our minds, the easier it is to believe everything we think. When we're stressed and anxious, believing our thoughts isn't helpful. Getting out and being social with supportive, nonjudgmental people goes a long way toward alleviating some of that stress, but for many children, offering kindness to others is also a powerful tool.

Altruistic acts can be as simple as holding the door for another student who is on crutches or offering to cover the difference when the person in front of you at the coffee shop is a few cents short. They can be more elaborate, such as tutoring younger students or participating in community service projects. Evidence shows that the kinder we are to others, the more forgiving we are of ourselves, and the happier we are. Often, all it takes is a few small kindnesses to remind us how good it feels to help others.

> **ACTIVITY: Weekly Gifts**
>
> Put slips of paper with the names of each member of your household into a hat or bowl. Designate one time per week when each person selects a slip of paper with someone else's name on it. You can keep it a secret or share the name you chose. In the next week, everyone has to perform one act of kindness for that person, and then everyone chooses again. Examples of things to do are:
>
> - Taking their turn with the dishes
> - Folding a load of their laundry
> - Making a cup of tea for them just the way they like it
> - Letting them have first chance at the shower without arguing
>
> Be as creative as you want to. Along with the obvious benefit of knowing that you will receive at least one act of kindness this week, this exercise focuses our attention outside ourselves and prompts us to really notice the other people in our household. You could find yourself asking, "How can I help _____ most today?"

This is a powerful way to build empathy and understanding among family members, as what is important and kind to one person might be very different to another. The trick is to do something they would appreciate, not necessarily what you'd like to receive.

REMIND THEM OF THEIR BEST ATTRIBUTES

Adolescents are constantly faced with feedback about where they fall short, and it can be exhausting to think that you never quite measure up. As a parent, it can sometimes be hard to keep our children' strengths and best qualities front of mind because we are so focused on making sure they're safe and making good choices. The following activity is a good way to help them frame their best attributes, and I love posting it on a bathroom mirror or closet door as a daily reminder of just how great my children are.

ACTIVITY: Skill Mapping

Traits and Passions—Is your child really interested in social justice? Teaching young people sports? Is she funny and artistic, or serious and academic? Ask her to spend some time thinking about how she would describe herself to someone who doesn't know her.

Self-Assessment—What is your child's assessment of his place in the world? His worth and value? What does he bring to the family and their friendships?

Skills/Knowledge—What does your child know a lot about: trains, dinosaurs, soccer, Minecraft? What does your child know innately? Is she in tune with others' emotions or able to read a room when she walks in to see what's happening? What are her unique skill sets?

Core Competencies—Maybe your child has an amazing set of study skills or puts people at ease. Maybe he is talented musically or able to remain calm in a scary situation. What are the core things he is good at?

Challenges—Part of knowing what we're good at is knowing where we struggle. Can your child identify the kinds of things she tends to find overwhelming or complicated? Can she identify people who are good at those things who she can rely on for support?

ENCOURAGE GRATITUDE

Because of the way the human brain is wired, we tend to focus on the negative things in our lives much more than the positive ones. Fortunately, the more we practice gratitude, the easier it gets, even if we start noticing things to be grateful for when things are going well in our lives.

I began my own gratitude practice as a way to ward off depression. When I was wrestling with stress and anxiety, mornings were my worst time. I often woke up, opening one eye at a time as I tried to determine whether a truckload of pain and longing was headed for me before my feet hit the floor. A friend suggested that I start making a list of things for which I was grateful before I ever opened my eyes in the morning, as a sort of shield against the barrage of negative thoughts with which I usually started my day. I figured it couldn't hurt.

In the beginning, it was hard to come up with much, not because I don't have many, many blessings in my life, but because I tend to qualify them. As soon as I thought of one, I either compared it to someone else's life and felt guilty that mine was easier than most, or I determined that it sounded silly and petty.

It took me a while to figure out that gratitude has nothing to do with comparisons. Gratitude doesn't start with "at least I'm not . . ." If I'm comparing my life to someone else's or thinking about all the ways things could be worse, I'm not creating positive thoughts. I'm creating negative ones masquerading as positive ones.

Gratitude also isn't a balance sheet. Please don't weigh the "good" things in your life against the "bad" ones and expect a tipping point at which your life is magical and wonderful. Gratitude stands on its own. And this might make it sound like it's a hard thing to do, but once you get going, it isn't.

Now, when I am frustrated or irritable, I've learned to take a deep breath and look around and be present where I am. I see my computer and am grateful for the ability to use it to connect with other people and learn really cool things. I catch sight of a glass of water and thank goodness for clean water to drink and bathe in. I see my sunglasses lying on the counter and smile at the thought of warm sunshine on my back. If I don't try to think beyond those things or conjure up stories in my head about them, just taking a few minutes to focus on the pure sensation of gratitude, I generally feel much better.

ACTIVITY: Daily Gratitude Practice

When my oldest daughter started high school, she began to struggle with anxiety. She was attending a school where she knew nobody, and the culture was very different from the school she had attended previously. She felt nervous, out of place, and a bit lonely. Pretty soon, she was asking to stay home, skip first period, or be picked up early. So, we started a gratitude practice.

Every night before she fell asleep, I asked her to text me three things for which she was grateful. If she was having a hard time coming up with anything, I texted her my list of three first. They were pretty basic—flannel sheets, a soft pillow, the dog snoring at the foot of the bed, remembering a joke the two of us had shared earlier. Within a week, she was texting me her three things without any prompting, and they gradually became more insightful and meaningful.

I had her text me for two reasons: first, I knew that she would be more comfortable sharing if we weren't face to face; and second, it didn't encourage conversation or any sort of judgment about her choices or mine. But maybe the best part of it was that, as she lay in bed texting me as her last act of the day, the final thoughts in her head were grateful, happy ones. It turned out to be a pretty powerful way to end the day and slip into rest.

None of these activities or ideas is meant to be a substitute for counseling or intervention by trained medical professionals. If your child is struggling with stress and anxiety to the point of being unable to focus or find meaning or joy, please seek professional help.

About the Author

Kari O'Driscoll holds bachelor's degrees in biology and philosophy from Pacific University in Oregon. She has worked in physical and mental health settings as well as schools and writes about social justice issues, parenting, mental health, and medical ethics. Her work has appeared in online journals and print anthologies, and she is the author of the social-emotional learning textbook *One Teenager at a Time: Building Self-Awareness and Critical Thinking in Adolescence* and a memoir titled *Truth Has a Different Shape*. Kari is active in her community, volunteering with the food bank and on the board of a local nonprofit, and is the mother of two strong, clever, compassionate daughters. Mostly, she is on a mission to let teenagers everywhere know that, despite the bad rap they often get, they are amazing.

www.ingramcontent.com/pod-product-compliance
Lightning Source LLC
Chambersburg PA
CBHW030146240426
43672CB00005B/289